Collins

KS3
Maths
Year 8

T0321492

Leisa Bovey, Ama Dickson and
Katherine Pate

How to use this book

Each Year 8 topic is presented on a two-page spread

Organise your knowledge with concise explanations and examples

Key points highlight fundamental ideas

Notes help to explain the mathematical steps

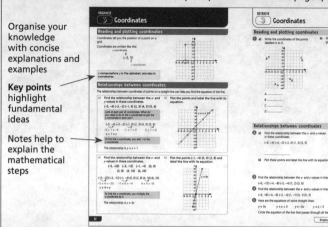

Test your retrieval skills by trying the accompanying questions for the topic

Mixed questions further test retrieval skills after all topics have been covered

Key facts and vocabulary section helps to consolidate knowledge of mathematical terms and concepts

Answers are provided to all questions at the back of the book

ACKNOWLEDGEMENTS

The authors and publisher are grateful to the copyright holders for permission to use quoted materials and images.

Every effort has been made to trace copyright holders and obtain their permission for the use of copyright material. The authors and publisher will gladly receive information enabling them to rectify any error or omission in subsequent editions. All facts are correct at time of going to press.

All images ©Shutterstock and HarperCollins*Publishers*

Published by Collins
An imprint of HarperCollins*Publishers* Limited
1 London Bridge Street
London SE1 9GF

HarperCollins*Publishers*
Macken House
39/40 Mayor Street Upper
Dublin 1
D01 C9W8
Ireland

© HarperCollins*Publishers* Limited 2023

ISBN 9780008598655

First published 2023

10 9 8 7 6 5 4 3

British Library Cataloguing in Publication Data.

A CIP record of this book is available from the British Library.

Authors: Leisa Bovey, Ama Dickson and Katherine Pate
Publisher: Clare Souza
Commissioning and Project Management: Richard Toms
Inside Concept Design and Layout: Ian Wrigley and Nicola Lancashire
Cover Design: Sarah Duxbury
Production: Emma Wood
Printed and bound in the UK

MIX
Paper | Supporting responsible forestry
FSC
www.fsc.org
FSC™ C007454

This book contains FSC™ certified paper and other controlled sources to ensure responsible forest management.

For more information visit: www.harpercollins.co.uk/green

Contents

Significant figures

What are significant figures?

The most **significant figure** (s.f.) is the digit with the **highest place value** in a number.

Significant figures are counted left to right from the highest non-zero place value.	A zero in between two other digits is also significant.	For numbers between 0 and 1, count significant figures from the first non-zero digit.
186 has 3 significant figures	**307 has 3 significant figures**	**0.0823 has 3 significant figures**

Hundreds	Tens	Ones
1	8	6

1st s.f. 2nd s.f. 3rd s.f.

Hundreds	Tens	Ones
3	0	7

1st s.f. 2nd s.f. 3rd s.f.

Ones	•	tenths	hundredths	thousandths	ten thousandths
0	•	0	8	2	3

1st s.f. 2nd s.f. 3rd s.f.

Rounding integers to significant figures

To round a number means to write an approximate value. A rounded number is less accurate, but often simpler to work with.

Remember the rules of rounding. 'Round up' if the digit to the right of the desired place value is greater than or equal to 5.

Round 384 to the nearest hundred.

Look at the hundreds values greater than and less than 384 and decide which value it is closer to.

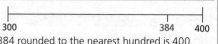

300   384   400

384 rounded to the nearest hundred is 400.

Rounding to a given number of significant figures means rounding to a certain number of digits rather than to a certain place value or number of decimal places. To round a number to a given number of significant figures, count the number of digits from the highest place value and round to the place value of the desired digit.

a)   Round 324 to 1 s.f.

Hundreds	Tens	Ones
3	2	4

The first significant figure is in the hundreds place, so rounding to 1 s.f. means to the nearest hundred.

324 rounded to 1 s.f. is 300

b)   Round 4852 to 2 s.f.

Thousands	Hundreds	Tens	Ones
4	8	5	2

The second significant figure is in the hundreds place, so rounding to 2 s.f. means to the nearest hundred.

4852 rounded to 2 s.f. is 4900

c)   Round 78 to 3 s.f.

Tens	Ones	•	tenths
7	8	•	0

The number 78 only has 2 significant figures. To write it to 3 s.f., fill in the third significant figure with a 0.

78 rounded to 3 s.f. is 78.0

Rounding decimal numbers to significant figures

Rounding numbers with decimals is the same as rounding integers. The exception is with numbers between 0 and 1, in which case the first significant figure is the first non-zero digit.

a)   Round 0.00649 to 1 s.f.

The first significant figure is in the thousandths place, so rounding to 1 s.f. means to the nearest thousandth.

0.00649 to 1 s.f. is 0.006

b)   Round 1.2093 to 3 s.f.

The third significant figure is in the hundredths place, so rounding to 3 s.f. means to the nearest hundredth.

1.2093 to 3 s.f. is 1.21

c)   Round 0.5021 to 2 s.f.

The second significant figure is in the hundredths place, so rounding to 2 s.f. means to the nearest hundredth.

0.5021 to 2 s.f. is 0.50

0.5 would only be to 1 s.f.

1 Significant figures

What are significant figures?

1 Underline the digit that is the third significant figure in the following numbers.

68124	9439	70623
0.00573	0.9406	0.10904

Rounding integers to significant figures

2 Round these numbers to the given number of significant figures.

	1 s.f.	2 s.f.	3 s.f.
57271			
843913759			
83			
1095			
165878			
2475000			

Rounding decimal numbers to significant figures

3 Round these numbers to the given number of significant figures.

	1 s.f.	2 s.f.	3 s.f.
0.23696			
0.059218			
1.056			
0.008			
9.976			
52.601			

Estimating calculations by rounding and limits of accuracy

Estimating calculations, including in real-life situations

Estimating is rounding **before** doing the calculation rather than after.

Imagine you are at an ice cream van and want to make sure you have enough cash for your order. Instead of adding up each item's exact price, you can round and estimate instead.

Ice lolly:
£2.95
Sundae:
£4.90

For two ice lollies, you could round each to £3, then 2 × £3 = £6. This is an **overestimate** – it is more than the actual price.

You will often need to estimate to the nearest power of 10 (e.g. 10, 100, or 1000), to 1 s.f., or to the nearest measurement.

$\frac{(21.7 \times 11.5) + 9.8}{10.1} = ?$

a) Estimate the answer to the calculation by rounding each number to 1 s.f.

21.7 is 20 to 1 s.f.   11.5 is 10 to 1 s.f.
9.8 is 10 to 1 s.f.   10.1 is 10 to 1 s.f.

$\frac{(21.7 \times 11.5) + 9.8}{10.1} \approx \frac{(20 \times 10) + 10}{10} \approx \frac{210}{10} = 21$

b) Calculate the actual answer.

$\frac{(21.7 \times 11.5) + 9.8}{10.1} = 25.68$ to 2 d.p.

c) Is the estimate an overestimate or an underestimate?

It is an underestimate as 21 is less than 25.68

Banana..................14p   Pepper...................78p
Apple.....................42p   Carrot......................6p
Orange..................37p
·Cash only·

a) Kian wants to buy 3 apples, 2 bananas and 4 carrots. By rounding to the nearest 5p, estimate the total.

42p apple rounded to the nearest 5p is 40p.
14p banana rounded to the nearest 5p is 15p.
6p carrot rounded to the nearest 5p is 5p.

(40p × 3) + (15p × 2) + (5p × 4)
= 120p + 30p + 20p = 170p = £1.70

b) Find the actual total.

(42p × 3) + (14p × 2) + (6p × 4)
= 126p + 28p + 24p = 178p = £1.78

c) Is the estimate an overestimate or an underestimate?

It is an underestimate.

It is less than the actual value as the prices of the apples and carrots have been rounded down by more than the bananas have been rounded up.

Accuracy

Nothing can be measured exactly. It is measured to a certain degree of accuracy. Even if the degree of accuracy is very small, it is not an exact measurement.

The degree of accuracy can be inferred by the way the measurement is written. For example, a measurement of 167 cm was recorded to the nearest cm while a measurement of 1.2 cm was recorded to the nearest tenth of a cm, or mm.

A measurement can also be expressed using **error intervals** to show the possible values it could be. A table measured as 167 cm won't be **exactly** 167 cm.

Numbers greater than 166.5 round to 167.

166.5 also rounds to 167, so use an 'or equal to' symbol, ≤. This is the **lower bound**, i.e. 166.5 is the absolute smallest the actual measurement could be in order to be rounded to 167.

Numbers less than 167.5 also round to 167.

However, 167.5 itself rounds to 168, so use a strictly 'less than' symbol, <. This is the **upper bound**, as it means all numbers **up to** 167.5.

To write the bounds in error interval notation:

166.5 cm ≤ length of table < 167.5 cm

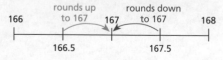

rounds up
to 167
166   167   168
166.5   167.5
rounds down
to 167

A quick way to find the bounds is to divide the degree of accuracy by 2. Then subtract that from the measurement to find the lower bound and add it to the measurement to find the upper bound.

Estimating calculations by rounding and limits of accuracy

Estimating calculations, including in real-life situations

1 Estimate the answer to the calculation by rounding to the given amount. Before calculating, decide whether rounding will give an overestimate or an underestimate. Give your estimate as a fraction if appropriate.

$$108.3 \div 6.24 =$$

a) **i)** Estimate the calculation by rounding to 1 significant figure.

....

ii) Will this be an overestimate or an underestimate?

....

b) **i)** Estimate the calculation by rounding to the nearest integer.

....

ii) Will this be an overestimate or an underestimate?

....

c) Use a calculator to find the actual value of the calculation.

....

2 Sophia orders two lattes, one hot chocolate and three teas for her friends. The prices are shown.

COFFEE CORNER

Latte £3.97
Hot chocolate £2.95
Tea £3.17
Flavoured syrup...£0.23

a) **i)** Estimate the total cost of Sophia's order by rounding to the nearest integer.

....

ii) Will this be an overestimate or an underestimate?

....

b) Use a calculator to find the actual cost of her order.

....

Accuracy

3 Write these measurements using error interval notation. Each is measured to the nearest unit.

a) The height of a jug measured to be 32 cm

....

b) The volume of milk in a glass measured to be 107 ml

....

c) The distance from London to Boston measured as 5264 km

....

② Introducing sequences

What is a sequence?

A **sequence** is a pattern of numbers or images appearing in a special order. The numbers in a sequence are called terms. An ellipsis (…) at the end of the sequence shows that it continues.

One more block is added each time

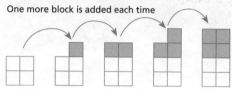

In an **arithmetic sequence** (also called a **linear sequence**), the terms increase or decrease by the same value (the **common difference**) each time.

1, 3, 5, 7, 9, … is an arithmetic sequence in which each term increases by 2.

25, 20, 15, 10, 5, … is an arithmetic sequence in which each term decreases by 5.

In a **geometric sequence**, each term is multiplied or divided to get the next term. The number the terms are multiplied or divided by is called the **common ratio**.

2, 4, 8, 16, 32, … is a geometric sequence in which each term is multiplied by 2 to get the next term.

> If a sequence is arithmetic, it is increasing or decreasing by a constant value.

Describing and generating arithmetic sequences

An arithmetic sequence can be described in words or by giving the **first term** and the common difference, or **term-to-term rule**.

$$2, \quad 8, \quad 14, \quad 20, \quad 26, \quad …$$
$+6 \quad +6 \quad +6 \quad +6$
1st term

Common difference +6

$$100, \quad 90, \quad 80, \quad 70, \quad 60, \quad …$$
$-10 \quad -10 \quad -10 \quad -10$
1st term

Common difference −10

To **generate a sequence** means to write down the terms. You need the first term and the relationship between the terms (the term-to-term rule).

The first term of a sequence is 15 and the value of each term is 4 less than the previous term. Generate the first five terms.

1st term is 15

2nd term is 15 − 4 = 11

3rd term is 11 − 4 = 7

4th term is 7 − 4 = 3

5th term is 3 − 4 = −1

The sequence is 15, 11, 7, 3, −1, …

> This is an arithmetic sequence as each term is decreasing by the same value.

Describing and generating other sequences

A **geometric sequence** can be described by stating the first term and the number each term is multiplied (or divided) by to get the next term.

The sequence 1, 4, 16, 64, … starts with 1 and each term is multiplied by 4 to create the next term.

Some sequences are neither arithmetic nor geometric. In the **Fibonacci sequence**, the previous two terms are added together to create the next term. The first eight terms in the sequence are:

1, 1, 2, 3, 5, 8, 13, 21

> 1 + 1 = 2, 1 + 2 = 3, 2 + 3 = 5, 3 + 5 = 8, etc.

The first term of a sequence is 100 and each term is half the previous term. Write the first five terms.

1st term is 100

2nd term is 100 ÷ 2 = 50

3rd term is 50 ÷ 2 = 25

4th term is 25 ÷ 2 = 12.5

5th term is 12.5 ÷ 2 = 6.25

The sequence is 100, 50, 25, 12.5, 6.25, …

> This is a geometric sequence as each term is being divided by 2.

> Any sequence can be written if you know how it starts and the relationship between the terms.

② Introducing sequences

What is a sequence?

1 Identify whether the following sequences are **arithmetic** or **geometric**. Circle your answers.

a) 2, 10, 50, 250, 1250   Arithmetic   Geometric

b) 6, 1, −4, −9, −14   Arithmetic   Geometric

c) 2, 4, 6, 8, 10   Arithmetic   Geometric

d) 16, 8, 4, 2, 1   Arithmetic   Geometric

Describing and generating arithmetic sequences

2 Describe each sequence by stating the first term and the common difference.

a) 7, 12, 17, 22, 27, …

b) 11, 7, 3, −1, −5, …

3 Write down the first five terms of each sequence.

a) First term 77, common difference −7

b) First term −6, common difference +3

Describing and generating other sequences

4 Describe each geometric sequence by stating the first term and the relationship between the terms.

a) 3, 9, 27, 81, 243, …

b) 54, 18, 6, 2, $\frac{2}{3}$, …

5 Write down the first five terms of a sequence with first term −1, multiplying each term by 3.

2 n^{th} term rules

Generating sequences from n^{th} term rules

The nth **term** rule (or **position-to-term rule**) describes a sequence and can be used to find any term, n, given its position in the sequence.

14, 11, 8, 5, 2

1st term	2nd term	3rd term	4th term	5th term
$n = 1$	$n = 2$	$n = 3$	$n = 4$	$n = 5$

The nth term rule for an arithmetic sequence will always be some number multiplied by n, plus (or minus) another number. The number multiplied by n is the common difference.

$$n^{th} \text{ term} = \boxed{}n + \boxed{}$$

common difference   a constant

To use the nth term rule, substitute the term number into the formula and find the value of the term.

> If given the rule, you can generate any sequence by substituting the term numbers (or positions) into the nth term rule.

To write the first five terms of an arithmetic sequence with the nth term rule $3n + 4$, substitute the values $n = 1, 2, 3, 4$ and 5 into the rule.

1st term: $n = 1$	$(3 \times 1) + 4 = 7$
2nd term: $n = 2$	$(3 \times 2) + 4 = 10$
3rd term: $n = 3$	$(3 \times 3) + 4 = 13$
4th term: $n = 4$	$(3 \times 4) + 4 = 16$
5th term: $n = 5$	$(3 \times 5) + 4 = 19$

The sequence is 7, 10, 13, 16, 19, ...

The nth term rule can be used to find any term of the sequence.

100th term: $n = 100$ $(3 \times 100) + 4 = 304$

> **Find the 1st, 2nd, 3rd and 20th terms of the sequence with n^{th} term rule $n^2 + 2n$**
>
> | | |
> |---|---|
> | 1st term: $n = 1$ | $1^2 + (2 \times 1) = 3$ |
> | 2nd term: $n = 2$ | $2^2 + (2 \times 2) = 8$ |
> | 3rd term: $n = 3$ | $3^2 + (2 \times 3) = 15$ |
> | 20th term: $n = 20$ | $20^2 + (2 \times 20) = 440$ |

Writing n^{th} term rules for arithmetic sequences

Follow these steps to find the nth term rule of an arithmetic sequence:

1. Find the common difference.
2. Write the common difference as the coefficient of n.
3. Substitute $n = 1$ into the expression from step 2 and find the constant. What needs to be added or subtracted to get the first term? Check by substituting another term.
4. Write the nth term rule using the common difference and the constant.

> **Find the nth term rule of the sequence 3, 5, 7, 9, 11, ...**
>
> First find the common difference.
>
> 3, 5, 7, 9, 11, ...
>   +2 +2 +2 +2
>
> The common difference is +2.
>
> Then write the common difference as the coefficient of n.
>
> The coefficient of n is +2 so write $2n$.
>
> Substitute $n = 1$.
>
> When $n = 1$, $2n$ is $2 \times 1 = 2$
>
> To get the first term of 3, add 1.
>
> When $n = 2$, $2n$ is $2 \times 2 = 4$
>
> To get the second term of 5, add 1.
>
> The constant is +1.
>
> Finally, write the nth term rule using the common difference and the constant.
>
> Common difference
> n^{th} term = $2n + 1$
> The constant

2 n^{th} term rules

Generating sequences from n^{th} term rules

1 Find the 1st, 2nd, 3rd and 10th terms of these sequences from the nth term rules.

a) $4n + 9$

....

b) $2n - 5$

....

2 Find the 1st, 2nd, 3rd and 10th terms of these sequences from the nth term rules.

a) $n^2 + 5$

....

b) $n^3 - 1$

....

Writing n^{th} term rules for arithmetic sequences

3 Find the nth term rule for these arithmetic sequences.

a) 1, 5, 9, 13, 17, ...

....

b) 22, 17, 12, 7, 2, ...

....

③ Coordinates

Reading and plotting coordinates

Coordinates tell you the position of a point on a grid.

Coordinates are written like this:

x-coordinate
↓

$(-3, 5)$

↑
y-coordinate

> x comes before y in the alphabet, and also in coordinates.

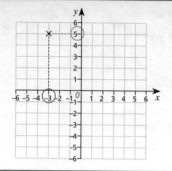

Relationships between coordinates

The relationships between coordinates of points on a straight line can help you find the equation of the line.

a) Find the relationship between the x- and y-values in these coordinates.

$(-5, -4)$ $(-3, -2)$ $(-1, 0)$ $(2, 3)$ $(4, 5)$ $(5, 6)$

> Look at each pair of coordinates. What do you need to do to the x-coordinate to get the y-coordinate in each pair?

$(-5, -4)$ $(-3, -2)$ $(-1, 0)$ $(2, 3)$ $(4, 5)$ $(5, 6)$

$-5 + 1 = -4$ $-1 + 1 = 0$ $5 + 1 = 6$
$x + 1 = y$

> To find the y-coordinate, you add 1 to the x-coordinate.

The relationship is $y = x + 1$

b) Plot the points and label the line with its equation.

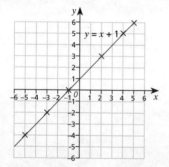

a) Find the relationship between the x- and y-values in these coordinates.

$(-5, -20)$ $(-3, -12)$ $(-1, -4)$ $(0, 0)$
$(2, 8)$ $(4, 16)$ $(6, 24)$

$(-5, -20)$ $(-3, -12)$ $(-1, -4)$ $(0, 0)$ $(2, 8)$ $(4, 16)$ $(6, 24)$

$-5 \times 4 = -20$ $-1 \times 4 = -4$ $4 \times 4 = 16$
$x \times 4 = y$

> To find the y-coordinate, you multiply the x-coordinate by 4.

The relationship is $y = 4x$

b) Plot the points $(-1, -4)$ $(0, 0)$ $(2, 8)$ and label the line with its equation.

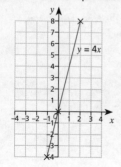

Coordinates

Reading and plotting coordinates

1 **a)** Write the coordinates of the points labelled A to D.

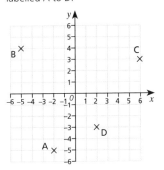

A ....

B ....

C ....

D ....

b) Plot and label these points on the coordinate grid.

E (7, –3)   F (–5, 0)   G (–1, 3)   H (3, 2)

i) Join points E to F to G to H to E with straight lines.

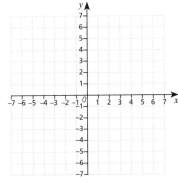

ii) Name the shape you have drawn.

....

Relationships between coordinates

2 **a)** Find the relationship between the x- and y-values in these coordinates.

(–6, –4) (–4, –2) (–2, 0) (1, 3) (3, 5)

....

b) Plot these points and label the line with its equation.

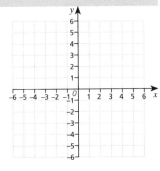

3 Find the relationship between the x- and y-values in these coordinates.

(–6, –12) (–4, –8) (–2, –4) (1, 2) (3, 6) ....

4 Find the relationship between the x- and y-values in these coordinates.

(–6, –8) (–4, –6) (–2, –4) (1, –1) (3, 1) (5, 3) ....

5 Here are the equations of some straight lines:

$y = 3x$ $y = x + 3$ $y = –3x$ $y = x – 3$

Circle the equation of the line that passes through all these points: (–5, 15) (0, 0) (2, –6)

Finding gradients

Gradient measures the **steepness** of a line.

Positive gradient   Negative gradient   Gradient = 0

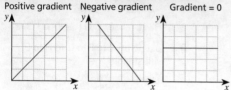

To find the gradient of a line, follow these steps:
- Decide if it is positive or negative.
- Draw a right-angled triangle.
- Label the change in x and change in y.
- Work out $\frac{\text{change in } y}{\text{change in } x}$

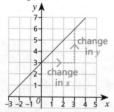

Calculate the gradient of each line.

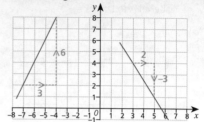

Gradient positive:
Gradient = $\frac{6}{3}$ = 2

Gradient negative:
Gradient = $\frac{-3}{2}$
        = $-\frac{3}{2}$ or −1.5

Parallel lines have the same gradient.

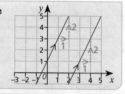

Drawing a line with a given gradient

The gradient tells you how far the line goes up (or down) for every square you move to the right.

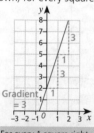

Gradient = 3

For every 1 square right, the line goes 3 up.

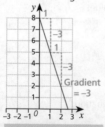

Gradient = −3

For every 1 square right, the line goes 3 down.

Draw a line with gradient 4 through point (2, 0).

Draw a cross at (2, 0). Gradient 4 means for every 1 across, go up 4.

Join the points with a straight line.

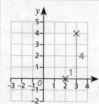

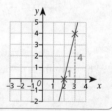

The grid shows two sides of a parallelogram.
Work out the coordinates of its fourth vertex.

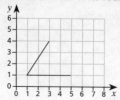

Draw lines parallel to the two sides.

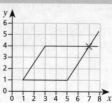

The fourth vertex is (7, 4).

③ Gradient

Finding gradients

1 Calculate the gradient of each line.

a)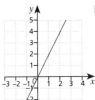

b)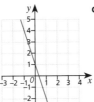

c)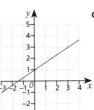

d)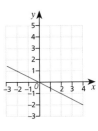

....

Drawing a line with a given gradient

2 Draw: **a)**   line A with gradient 3 through the point (0, −1)

         b)   line B with gradient −2 through the point (0, 3)

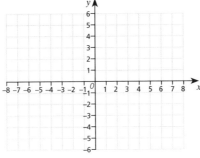

3 The diagram shows three vertices (labelled A, B, C) of a rectangle.

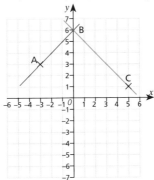

a)   Calculate the gradients of AB and BC.   AB: ....   BC: ....

b)   Work out the coordinates of the fourth vertex of the rectangle.

                                                   ....

Drawing graphs of equations like $y = 2$ and $x = -4$

On the line with equation $y = 2$, all the points have y-coordinate 2.

On the line with equation $x = -4$, all the points have x-coordinate -4.

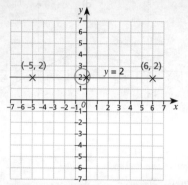

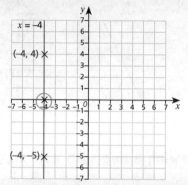

Drawing a graph from a table of values

To draw the graph of an equation:
- Make a table of values.

x	−4	−2	0	1	3
y					

- Substitute each x-value into the equation and work out the corresponding y-value.
- Plot the (x, y) pairs on a coordinate grid, and join them.

Draw the graph of $y = 2x - 3$ for values of x between -2 and 5.

Make a table of values:

$y = 2x - 3$ x-values between −2 and 5

x	−2	−1	0	3	5
y	−7	−5	−3	3	7

When $x = -2$,
$y = 2x - 3$
$y = 2 \times -2 - 3$
$y = -4 - 3$
$y = -7$
$(-2, -7)$

When $x = 0$,
$y = 2x - 3$
$y = 2 \times 0 - 3$
$y = 0 - 3$
$y = -3$
$(-1, -5)$ $(0, -3)$

When $x = 5$,
$y = 2x - 3$
$y = 2 \times 5 - 3$
$y = 10 - 3$
$y = 7$
$(3, 3)$ $(5, 7)$

Plot the points on the coordinate grid.

Join them with a straight line.

Label the graph with its equation.

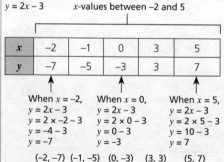

Graphing linear equations

Drawing graphs of equations like $y = 2$ and $x = -4$

1 Draw and label the graphs of $x = -5$, $x = 3$ and $x = 6$

2 Draw and label the graphs of $y = -6$, $y = 1$ and $y = 3$

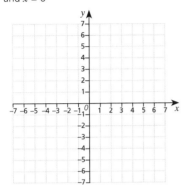

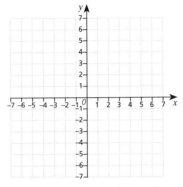

Drawing a graph from a table of values

3 Draw the graph of $y = 3x + 1$ for values of x between -3 and 2.

x	−3	−1	0	1	2
y	−8				

4 Draw the graph of $y = 2 - x$ for values of x between -4 and 4.

x	−4				4
y					

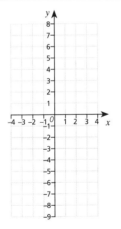

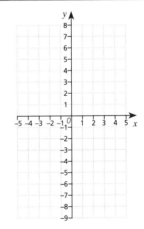

3 $y = mx + c$

Finding parallel lines

The equation of a straight line is:

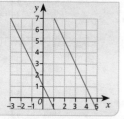

$$y = mx + c$$

with gradient (pointing to m) and y-intercept (pointing to c).

Parallel lines have the same gradient.

Here are the equations of four straight lines.

$y = 4x + 5$ $\quad$ $y = x + 4$ $\quad$ $3y - 12x = 1$ $\quad$ $y + 4x = 10$

Which two lines are parallel?

Rearrange $3y - 12x = 1$ and $y + 4x = 10$ to $y = mx + c$

$3y - 12x = 1$	$y + 4x = 10$
$3y = 12x + 1$	$y = -4x + 10$
$y = 4x + \frac{1}{3}$	

Look for the equations with the same m value.

$y = ④x + 5$ $\quad$ $y = x + 4$ $\quad$ $y = ④x + \frac{1}{3}$ $\quad$ $y = -4x + 10$
$\qquad\qquad\qquad\qquad\qquad (3y - 12x = 1)$ $\quad$ $(y + 4x = 10)$

$y = 4x + 5$ and $3y - 12x = 1$ are parallel.

Finding lines with the same y-intercept

Lines with the same y-intercept have the same c value. These lines all have a y-intercept of 2:

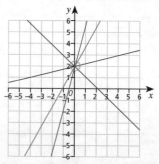

Here are the equations of four straight lines.

$y = 2x + 5$ $\quad$ $y = x - 5$ $\quad$ $5y - 4x = 20$ $\quad$ $y - 3x + 5 = 0$

Which two lines have the same y-intercept?

Rearrange $5y - 4x = 20$ and $y - 3x + 5 = 0$ to $y = mx + c$

$5y - 4x = 20$	$y - 3x + 5 = 0$
$5y = 4x + 20$	$y = 3x - 5$
$y = 0.8x + 4$	

Look for the equations with the same c value.

$y = 2x + 5$ $\quad$ $y = x ⊖ 5$ $\quad$ $y = 0.8x + 4$ $\quad$ $y = 3x ⊖ 5$

$y = x - 5$ and $y - 3x + 5 = 0$ have the same y-intercept.

Using the gradient and y-intercept to draw graphs

To draw the graph of $y = mx + c$:
- plot the point $(0, c)$
- draw a line through $(0, c)$ with gradient m.

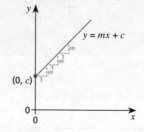

Draw the graph of $y = 2x - 3$

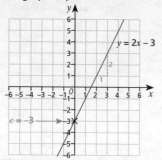

$y = mx + c$

Finding parallel lines

1 a) Rearrange the equations of these three straight lines into the form $y = mx + c$

i) $4y - 2x = 1$ **ii)** $y + 2x = 4$ **iii)** $y - 2x = 3$

....

b) Which of the lines in part a) is parallel to the line $y = 2x + 1$? ....

2 Here are the equations of four straight lines. $y = \frac{2}{5}x$ $5y + 2x = 4$ $4y - 3x = 5$ $5y = 3 - 2x$

Which two lines are parallel?

.... and ....

Finding lines with the same y-intercept

3 Complete this table for the straight lines with these equations.

Equation	Gradient	Coordinates of y-intercept
$y = 3x + 5$		
$y = -2x - 1$		
$y = 6x$		
$y = -3$		
$y = 2 - x$		
$2y = x - 7$		

4 Here are the equations of four straight lines. $y = -x + 2$ $y = x - 2$ $3y - 4x = 2$ $y - 3x - 2 = 0$

Which two lines have the same y-intercept?

.... and ....

Using the gradient and y-intercept to draw graphs

5 Draw the graph of $y = x + 3$

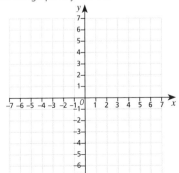

6 Draw the graph of $y = -2x - 1$

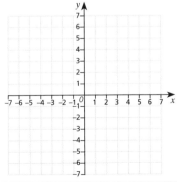

3 Linear relationships

Recognising linear relationships

When two quantities have a linear relationship, their graph is a straight line.

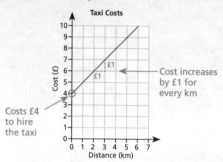

Costs £4 to hire the taxi

Cost increases by £1 for every km

The cost of a taxi ride and distance travelled have a linear relationship.

> When two quantities x and y have a linear relationship, their equation is in the form $y = mx + c$

Here are some coordinates:

$(-4, -1)$ $(0, 3)$ $(7, 10)$

Do they lie on a straight line?

> Find the relationship between the x- and y-values in the coordinates.

To find the y-coordinate, you add 3 to the x-coordinate.

Writing this as an equation gives $y = x + 3$

This is of the form $y = mx + c$, so the relationship is linear and the points lie on a straight line.

Finding the equation of a line

To find the equation of a line:
- find the y-intercept
- find the gradient
- substitute into $y = mx + c$

> The equation of a line is:
>
> gradient y-intercept
>
> $$y = mx + c$$

Find the equation of this line.

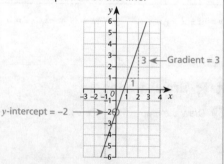

y-intercept = −2

Gradient = 3

Equation is $y = 3x - 2$

Find the equation for the cost c of a taxi in terms of distance travelled, d.

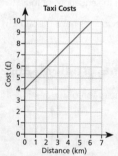

Intercept on cost axis = 4

Gradient = 1

Equation is $c = d + 4$

③ Linear relationships

Recognising linear relationships

1 For each set of coordinates, decide if they lie on a straight line.

If they do, write the equation of the line.

a) (−5, −10) (−2, −4) (3, 6) ....

b) (−3, 2) (2, 7) (−1, 4) ....

c) (−4, 12) (2, 6) (1, −3) ....

2 These coordinates all lie on a straight line: (−2, −6) (5, 8) (0, −2) (9, 16)

Circle the equation of this line.

$y = 2x - 1$ $y = 2(x - 1)$ $y = 3x$ $y = 2x$

Finding the equation of a line

3 Find the equations of these lines.

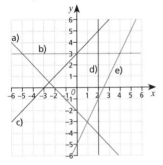

a) ....

b) ....

c) ....

d) ....

e) ....

4 The graph shows the cost of hiring a bike for different numbers of hours.

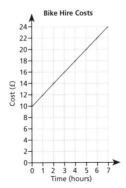

Find the equation for the cost c of hiring a bike in terms of time in hours, t.

....

④ Solving one-step equations

Equations and inverse operations

An expression is a collection of **terms** that can be **variables** or **constants** without an equals symbol.

An **equation** consists of one or more **expressions**. Both sides of the equation are equal in value (as shown by the = symbol).

A set of **balance scales** can help to visualise equations. This set of scales represents the equation $x + 2 = 5$.

To solve equations, you need to use **inverse operations** (these 'undo' other operations).

Inverse operations		
Addition +	⟺	Subtraction −
Multiplication ×	⟺	Division ÷
Powers (e.g. x^2, x^3)	⟺	Roots (e.g. $\sqrt{x}$, $\sqrt[3]{x}$)

Using visual aids to solve equations

To '**solve** for x' means to find the value of x. The x term must be **isolated** on one side of the equation. The aim is to get the variables to one side of the equation and the constants to the other.

This equation mat, scales and bar model all show the equation $x + 3 = 6$.

> Whatever you do to one side of the equation, you must do to the other to keep it balanced.

Algebraic steps	Equation mat	Scales	Bar model
Lay out the equation. $x + 3 = 6$			
Use inverse operations to isolate x. $x + 3 - 3 = 6 - 3$ Subtract 3 from both sides	Place three −1 tiles on both sides. The +1 and −1 tiles 'cancel out' because they add up to 0.	Remove 3 ones tiles from both sides.	'Cancel out' the parts that are the same on both bars.
Simplify $x = 3$			

Solving without visual aids

To solve an equation without visual aids, use inverses and carry out the same operation on both sides to keep it balanced like a set of scales.

$4x = 8$

The inverse of × 4 is ÷ 4, so divide both sides by 4.

$4x ÷ 4 = 8 ÷ 4$

$x = 2$

To check: $4 × 2 = 8$ ✔

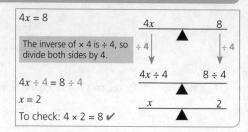

Solving one-step equations

Equations and inverse operations

1 Show each equation on a set of balance scales using algebra tiles.

a) $2x + 4 = 8$　　　　　　　　　**b)** $3x + 2 = 11$

Using visual aids to solve equations

2 Show $x + 6 = 8$ using algebra tiles and find the value of x.

$x =$ ....

Solving without visual aids

3 Solve the following equations for x.

a) $x + 9 = 15$　　　　　　**b)** $x \div 5 = 3$　　　　　　**c)** $12x = 96$

$x =$ ....　　　　$x =$ ....　　　　$x =$ ....

(4) Solving two-step equations

Using algebra tiles

Algebra tiles can help to visualise how to solve two-step equations.

> Use inverse operations to combine like terms so that all the variables are on one side of the equation and the constants on the other.

Consider $2x - 8 = 10$. There are 2 x tiles and 8 negative one tiles on the left-hand side. There are 10 positive one tiles on the right-hand side.

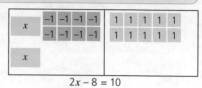

$2x - 8 = 10$

To get x on its own on one side of the equation, use inverse operations and add 8 to both sides.

Simplify by combining the ones tiles.

The 8 positive tiles 'cancel out' the 8 negative ones.

$2x - 8 + 8 = 10 + 8$
$2x = 18$

Now divide each side into two equal groups to find the value of $1x$.

Two x tiles equal 18, so one x tile equals 9.

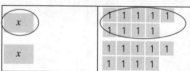

$2x \div 2 = 18 \div 2$
$x = 9$

To check: $2 \times 9 - 8 = 18 - 8 = 10$ ✔

Solving without visual aids

To solve two-step equations without visual aids, use inverse operations and write down each step. Carry out the same operation on both sides. To solve $2x - 8 = 10$ without algebra tiles, you can first divide by 2 (since all terms are divisible by 2) or you can add 8 to both sides.

$2x - 8 = 10$	Add 8 to both sides.
$+8 \quad +8$	
$2x = 18$	Divide both sides by 2.
$\div 2 \quad \div 2$	
$x = 9$	

$2x - 8 = 10$	Divide both sides by 2.
$\div 2 \quad \div 2$	
$x - 4 = 5$	Add 4 to both sides.
$+4 \quad +4$	
$x = 9$	

To solve $5x - 9 = 16$, it is not sensible to divide each term before solving because there is not a common factor between 5, 9 and 16.

$5x - 9 = 16$
$+9 \qquad +9$ Add 9 to both sides.

$5x = 25$ Simplify.

$\div 5 \qquad \div 5$ Divide both sides by 5.

$x = 5$

To check: $5 \times 5 - 9 = 25 - 9 = 16$ ✔

a) **Find the value of n in $3n - 5 = 31$**

$3n - 5 = 31$
$+5 \quad +5$ Add 5 to both sides.

$3n = 36$
$\div 3 \quad \div 3$ Divide both sides by 3.

$n = 12$

To check: $3 \times 12 - 5 = 36 - 5 = 31$ ✔

b) **Find the value of a in $\frac{a}{4} - 3 = 2$**

Remember that a fraction is another way of writing division, so $\frac{a}{4}$ means $a \div 4$.

$\frac{a}{4} - 3 = 2$
$+3 \quad +3$ Add 3 to both sides.

$\frac{a}{4} = 5$

$\frac{a}{4} \times 4 = 5 \times 4$ Multiply both sides by 4.

$a = 20$

To check: $\frac{20}{4} - 3 = (20 \div 4) - 3$
$= 5 - 3 = 2$ ✔

Solving two-step equations

Using algebra tiles

1. Show the equation $2x - 5 = 9$ using algebra tiles and solve for x.

   If you don't have algebra tiles to hand, you can instead cut up bits of paper and label them.

   $x =$ ....

Solving without visual aids

2. Solve each of the following equations. Show your working.

   a) $6x + 10 = 28$

   $x =$ ....

   b) $\frac{x}{2} + 3 = 6$

   $x =$ ....

   c) $5x - 4 = 41$

   $x =$ ....

   d) $\frac{x}{6} + 8 = 14$

   $x =$ ....

4 Solving equations with variables on both sides

Using bar models (when all terms are positive)

Bar models are a good way to visualise equations with variables on both sides of the equals symbol when all the terms are positive.

> A bar model doesn't work as well when there are negative terms. In that case, it is best to use algebra tiles.

This bar model shows the equation $5x + 1 = 2x + 7$:

x	x	x	x	x	1
x	x	1	1	1	1 1 1

To solve the equation, 'cancel out' the terms that are the same in both bars.

This leaves $3x = 6$, or $1x = 2$, so the answer is $x = 2$.

Using algebra tiles (when terms are positive and/or negative)

To solve equations with variables on both sides using algebra tiles, carry out inverse operations so that all the variable tiles are on one side of the equation and the constants are on the other.

> It doesn't matter if the variables are on the left or the right, as long as they are all on the same side.

These algebra tiles show the equation $6x - 2 = 3x + 7$	Get the variables on one side.	Isolate the x term then simplify.	Divide each side into three equal groups.
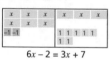 $6x - 2 = 3x + 7$	Add 3 $-x$ tiles to both sides and simplify 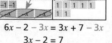 $6x - 2 - 3x = 3x + 7 - 3x$ $3x - 2 = 7$	Add 2 to both sides and simplify 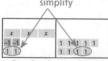 $3x - 2 + 2 = 7 + 2$ $3x = 9$	1 x tile equals 3 ones tiles  $3x \div 3 = 9 \div 3$ $x = 3$ To check, substitute $x = 3$ into $6x - 2 = 3x + 7$ $6 \times 3 - 2 = 18 - 2 = 16$ $3 \times 3 + 7 = 9 + 7 = 16$ ✔

Solving without visual aids

To solve $2y + 6 = 4y$, use inverse operations to get the y term on one side of the equation. In this case, subtracting $2y$ from both sides is easier because subtracting $4y$ would leave a negative y term, but both methods give the same answer:

$2y + 6 = 4y$
$2y + 6 - 2y = 4y - 2y$ Subtract 2y from both sides.
$6 = 2y$ Simplify.
$6 \div 2 = 2y \div 2$ Divide both sides by 2.
$3 = y$

$2y + 6 = 4y$
$2y + 6 - 4y = 4y - 4y$ Subtract 4y from both sides.
$-2y + 6 = 0$ Simplify.
$-2y + 6 - 6 = 0 - 6$ Subtract 6 from both sides.
$-2y = -6$ Simplify.
$-2y \div -2 = -6 \div -2$ Divide both sides by –2.
$y = 3$

To check the answer is correct, substitute $y = 3$ into $2y + 6 = 4y$

$2 \times 3 + 6 = 6 + 6 = 12$

$4 \times 3 = 12$ ✔

> Similarly, you could subtract 6 from both sides first or divide each term by 2 first and you would arrive at the same answer.

Solving equations with variables on both sides

Using bar models (when all terms are positive)

1 Draw bar models and solve the following equations.

a) $2x + 8 = 3x + 6$

b) $3b + 5 = 4b + 1$

$x = \text{................}$

$b = \text{................}$

Using algebra tiles (when terms are positive and/or negative)

2 Show the equation $4x + 6 = 6x - 4$ using algebra tiles. Then use the tiles or your preferred method to solve the equation. If you do not have algebra tiles to hand, you can cut up bits of paper and label them.

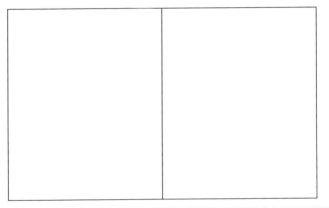

$x = \text{................}$

Solving without visual aids

3 Solve each of the following equations. Show your working.

a) $2x + 6 = 5x - 15$

$x = \text{................}$

b) $3x - 4 = 20 - x$

$x = \text{................}$

(4) Solving equations with brackets

Expanding brackets using the distributive law

The **distributive law** says that the product of two numbers multiplied together is equal to the product of those numbers split into groups (**partitioned**).

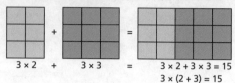

3×2 + 3×3 = $3 \times 2 + 3 \times 3 = 15$
$3 \times (2 + 3) = 15$

The distributive law can be shown without visual aids by **expanding the bracket**.

$3(2 + 3) = (3 \times 2) + (3 \times 3)$
$= 6 + 9$
$= 15$

The same rule applies when there are variables inside or outside the brackets. $5(2x + 3)$ can be expanded using an area model. Draw a large rectangle partitioned into smaller rectangles and find the area of each.

	$2x$	3
5	$10x$	15

$5 \times 2x$ 5×3

$5(2x + 3)$
$= (5 \times 2x) + (5 \times 3)$
$= 10x + 15$

To expand a pair of brackets with more than two terms, you must multiply by each term.

To expand $4(2x + 3y - 8)$, multiply 4 by each term in the bracket.

	$2x$	$3y$	-8
4	$8x$	$12y$	-32

$4 \times 2x$ $4 \times 3y$ 4×-8

$4(2x + 3y - 8)$
$= 8x + 12y - 32$

> **Multiply what is outside the brackets by everything inside the brackets.**

When expanding brackets, remember that:

* multiplying or dividing two negative numbers gives a positive number
* multiplying or dividing a negative and a positive gives a negative number
* adding a negative number is the same as subtracting
* subtracting a negative number is the same as adding.

$+ \times + = +$
$- \times - = +$
$- \times + = -$
$+ \times - = -$

> **Expand $3m(2 - 7n)$**
>
> Multiply $3m$ by each term inside the bracket and carry the negative sign through to the answer.
>
> $3m(2 - 7n) = (3m \times 2) + (3m \times - 7n)$
> $= 6m - 21mn$

Solving equations with brackets

To solve an equation with one pair of brackets, decide whether it will be easier to expand the brackets first or to divide by the number in front of the brackets.

> **Solve for k. $3(k - 5) = 6$**
>
> | | |
> |---|---|
> | $3 \times k + 3 \times -5 = 6$ | $3(k - 5) = 6$ |
> | $3k - 15 = 6$ | $\div 3 \quad \div 3$ |
> | $+15 \quad +15$ | $k - 5 = 2$ |
> | $3k = 21$ | $+5 \quad +5$ |
> | $\div 3 \quad \div 3$ | $k = 7$ |
> | $k = 7$ | |
>
> To check, substitute $k = 7$ into $3(k - 5) = 6$
> $3(7 - 5) = 3 \times 2 = 6$ ✔

If an equation has more than one pair of brackets, expand all the brackets and simplify before solving.

> **Solve $3(2j - 4) + 2(j + 3) = 26$**
>
> First expand both brackets.
>
> | $3(2j - 4)$ | $2(j + 3)$ |
> |---|---|
> | $= (3 \times 2j) + (3 \times - 4)$ | $= (2 \times j) + (2 \times 3)$ |
> | $= 6j - 12$ | $= 2j + 6$ |
>
> $6j - 12 + 2j + 6 = 26$
> $8j - 6 = 26$
> $+6 \quad +6$
> $8j = 32$
> $\div 8 \quad \div 8$
> $j = 4$

Solving equations with brackets

Expanding brackets using the distributive law

1 Expand each expression and simplify where possible by combining like terms.

a) $3(2k - 4) + 5k$ 　　　　　　**b)** $k(2m - 4)$ 　　　　　　**c)** $4(2x + 3y - 5)$

Solving equations with brackets

2 Solve the following equations.

a) $3(k - 5) = 12$

$k =$ ....

b) $2x + 3(4 - x) = 10$

$x =$ ....

3 Solve the following equations.

a) $2(x + 3) + 4(x - 5) = 10$

$x =$ ....

b) $5(y - 2) = 3(y - 2) + 2$

$y =$ ....

5 Multiplicative relationships

What is a multiplicative relationship?

The term **multiplicative relationship** refers to how two numbers are connected by multiplication. The number that links them is called a **multiplier**.

- 2 and 6 are in a multiplicative relationship because $2 \times 3 = 6$

  3 is the multiplier

- 4 and 3 are in a multiplicative relationship because $4 \times \frac{3}{4} = 3$

  $\frac{3}{4}$ is the multiplier

Any two numbers, a and b, are related by the multiplier $\frac{b}{a}$ because $a \times \frac{b}{a} = b$. To find the multiplier between a and b, divide b by a.

A graph of a multiplicative relationship is a straight line (linear) graph from the origin (0, 0).

This graph shows the equation $y = \frac{3}{4}x$. Every point on the line shows the multiplicative relationship.

The point (6, 4.5) shows the relationship from $x = 6$ to $y = 4.5$

$6 \times \frac{3}{4} = 4.5$

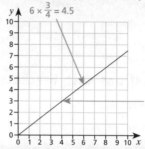

The point (4, 3) shows the relationship from $x = 4$ to $y = 3$.

$4 \times \frac{3}{4} = 3$

Currency and unit conversion

An exchange rate is a multiplier between currencies. For example, if the exchange rate between pounds (£) and euros (€) is given as £1 = €1.20, the multiplier is 1.2

To convert between currencies, multiply or divide by the value of the multiplier to find the unknown amount.

$$\times 1.2$$
£1 = €1.20

$$\div 1.2$$
€1.20 = £1

£1 = €1.20

a) Find £15 in €.

Setting up the problem using a ratio table can help you keep track of whether to divide or multiply.

× 1.2

£1	€1.20
£15	?

× 1.2

To convert £ to €, multiply by 1.2

$15 \times 1.2 = 18$

£15 is €18

b) Find €24 in £.

÷ 1.2

£1	€1.20
?	€24

÷ 1.2

To convert € to £, divide by 1.2

$24 \div 1.2 = 20$

€24 is £20

This graph shows the conversion between miles and kilometres.

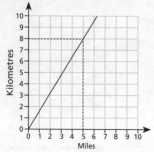

Calculate approximately how many kilometres are in 15 miles.

Find a point on the graph that is easy to read.

The point (5, 8) shows that 5 miles is 8 km.

To find the multiplier from miles to km, divide 8 by 5.

$8 \div 5 = \frac{8}{5}$

Next, multiply by the given distance.

$15 \times \frac{8}{5} = 24$

15 miles is approximately 24 km.

Multiplicative relationships

What is a multiplicative relationship?

1 Find the multiplier in each relationship.

a) $5 \times \dfrac{\square}{\square} = 12$ **b)** $8 \times \dfrac{\square}{\square} = 7$ **c)** $6 \times \square = 12$ **d)** $10 \times \dfrac{\square}{\square} = 8$

2 Which graph(s) show(s) a multiplicative relationship? Circle your answer(s).

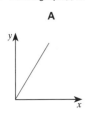

Currency and unit conversion

3 Ginny is going on holiday to the USA. The exchange rate is £1 = $1.47

a) Before her holiday, she converts £300 to US dollars ($).

How much does she receive in $?

b) Ginny returns from her holiday with $75 and converts it back into pounds (£) using the same exchange rate.

How much does she receive in £?

4 Use the conversion graph shown on page 30.

How many miles is 36 km?

Percentages

Fractions, decimals and percentages

Percent means '**out of 100**'. Percentages, fractions and decimals are all ways to represent part of a whole, so percentages can also be written as equivalent fractions and decimals.

57 out of 100 squares (57%) are shaded

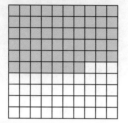

Write the amount of cake that has been eaten as a fraction, a decimal and a percentage.

3 out of 8 slices have been eaten. That means $\frac{3}{8}$ of the cake has been eaten.

$\frac{3}{8} = 3 \div 8$ $8\overline{\smash{)}3 \ . \ ^30 \ ^60 \ ^40}$ $\frac{3}{8} = 0.375$

$0.375 \times 100 = 37.5\%$

Conversion	Method
Decimal to percentage	Multiply by 100, e.g. $0.75 \times 100 = 75\%$
Decimal to fraction	Use the smallest decimal place value as the denominator and digits as the numerator, e.g. $0.7\underline{5} = \frac{75}{100} = \frac{3}{4}$ (Divide by 25 to simplify $\frac{75}{100}$). Hundredths place
Percentage to decimal	Divide by 100, e.g. $75\% \div 100 = 0.75$
Percentage to fraction	Use 100 as the denominator and the percentage as the numerator, e.g. $75\% = \frac{75}{100}$
Fraction to decimal	Divide the numerator by the denominator, e.g. $\frac{3}{4} = 3 \div 4$ $4\overline{\smash{)}3 \ . \ ^30 \ ^20}$ $\frac{3}{4} = 0.75$
Fraction to percentage	Convert to a decimal then multiply by 100, e.g. $\frac{3}{4} = 0.75$ $0.75 \times 100 = 75\%$

One number as a percentage of another number

To find what percent one number is of another, divide the first number by the second and multiply by 100.

7 out of 10 beads in a bag are red.

This is $\frac{7}{10}$ as a fraction. As a decimal, $\frac{7}{10} = 0.7$

$0.7 \times 100 = 70\%$, so 70% of the beads are red.

To find what percent 18 is of 12, divide $18 \div 12 = 1.5$, then $1.5 \times 100 = 150\%$. 18 is 150% of 12.

A shirt that originally cost £20 is reduced by £3 in a sale. By what percentage has the price decreased?

Find what percent £3 is of £20.

$\frac{3}{20} = 3 \div 20 = 0.15$, then $0.15 \times 100 = 15\%$

The price of the shirt has decreased by 15%.

Finding percentages of a number or an amount

To find a percentage of an amount, convert the percentage to a decimal or fraction and multiply by the amount.

This bar model shows finding 12% of £180.

£180

£?	£?
12%	88%

100%

To find 12% of £180, convert 12% to a decimal or fraction, then multiply by 180. 12% of £180 = £21.60

To find 10% of a number, × by 0.1, or ÷ by 10.

To find 5% of a number, halve 10% of the number.

To find 1% of a number, × by 0.01, or ÷ by 100.

Find 17% of 160.

10% of 160 = 160 ÷ 10 = 16
5% of 160 = 16 ÷ 2 = 8
2% of 160 = 1.6 × 2 = 3.2

17% of 160 =
10% of 160 +
5% of 160 +
2% of 160

So 17% of 160 = 16 + 8 + 3.2 = 27.2

⑤ Percentages

Fractions, decimals and percentages

1 Complete the table.

Fraction	$\frac{19}{50}$		
Decimal		0.74	
Percentage			
Diagram			

One number as a percentage of another number

2 Find the percent by which each of these items is discounted. Give your answers to the nearest percent.

a) A shirt is originally £18 and is decreased by £2.

b) A pair of trousers is originally £38 and is decreased by £5.

Finding percentages of a number or an amount

3 A theme park offers a discount of 8% for tickets bought online.
A family of 1 adult and 3 children plan to go to the theme park.

How much will they save by buying their tickets online?

'At the gate' prices

Adults £40
Children £19

5 Percentage changes

Percentage decrease

Prices may be reduced by a certain percentage; this is an example of **percentage decrease**.

This bar model represents a £530 TV decreased in price by 15%. £530 is 100% of the original cost. The price is reduced by 15%, so the sale price is 85% of the original.

£530

£?	£?
15%	85%

100%

To find the new price, either find 15% of the original price and subtract it from the original price, or find 85% of the original price.

To find the new price, use one of these methods:

Convert 15% to a decimal: 15% = 15 ÷ 100 = 0.15	Find the percentage the sale price is of the original price: 100% − 15% = 85%
Find the amount of the decrease: £530 × 0.15 = £79.50	Convert 85% to a decimal: 85% = 85 ÷ 100 = 0.85
Find the new price: £530 − £79.50 = £450.50	Find the new price: £530 × 0.85 = £450.50

> **To find the new value after a percentage decrease, multiply the original value by the percent remaining after the decrease (100% − percentage decrease).**

Percentage increase

Prices may rise by a certain percentage; this is called **percentage increase**. Interest in a bank account is also an example of percentage increase. The bank pays interest based on a percentage of the balance. When this interest is paid at the end of the year, it is called **simple interest**.

This bar model shows the interest earned on a £1500 bank account. The new balance is 2% more than at the start. So the new balance is 102% of the starting balance.

£?

£1500	£?
100%	2%

102%

To find the new balance, use one of these methods:

Convert 2% to a decimal: 2% = 2 ÷ 100 = 0.02	Find the percentage the new balance is of the original balance: 100% + 2% = 102%
Find the amount of interest earned: £1500 × 0.02 = £30	Convert 102% to a decimal: 102% = 102 ÷ 100 = 1.02
Add to the original balance to find the new balance: £1500 + £30 = £1530	Find the new balance: £1500 × 1.02 = £1530

> **To find the new value after a percentage increase, multiply the original value by (100% + the percentage increase).**

Finding the percentage change

The percentage by which a value has increased or decreased is the **percentage change**. It is the same as asking what percentage one number is of another.

> % change = $\frac{\text{amount of increase or decrease}}{\text{original value}} \times 100$

The price of a video game has been reduced by £5. The original price was £40.

% change = $\frac{\text{amount of increase or decrease}}{\text{original value}} \times 100$

% decrease = $\frac{5}{40} \times 100 = 12.5\%$

The price has decreased by 12.5%

Find the percentage increase in the amount of shampoo in the bottle.

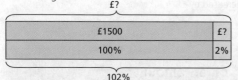

Amount of increase:

420 ml − 400 ml = 20 ml

% change = $\frac{\text{amount of increase or decrease}}{\text{original value}} \times 100$

% increase = $\frac{20}{400} \times 100 = 5\%$

The amount of shampoo has increased by 5%

Percentage changes

Percentage decrease

1 A furniture shop is having a sale. The original prices are shown.

Calculate the new price of each item.

a)

b)

Percentage increase

2 A manufacturer is increasing the amounts in its food packages.

a) Increase the amount of cereal by 8%

b) Increase the amount of porridge by 20%

Finding the percentage change

3 An electronics store is having a sale on TVs.

Calculate the percentage change of each of these discounts given the original prices indicated. Give your answers to the nearest percent.

a) A TV originally costs £2500 and is being discounted by £300.

b) A TV originally costs £1700 and is now £1350.

Repeated percentage change and finding the original value

Percentage multipliers

An efficient way of finding a new value after a percentage change is to multiply by the percentage the new value represents; this is called using a **multiplier**.

To find the mass after a 20% decrease from 200 g, recognise that a 20% decrease means that the new mass is 80% of the original. So multiply 200 × 0.8 = 160 g. The value 0.8 is the multiplier.

To find the volume after a 10% increase from 300 ml, recognise that a 10% increase means the new volume is 110% of the original. So multiply 300 × 1.1 = 330 ml. The value 1.1 is the multiplier.

Repeated percentage change

Repeated percentage change is when an amount is repeatedly changed by a percentage increase or decrease. For example, a bank may pay interest on a balance year after year, including on the interest earned in previous years; this is called **compound interest**.

£2000 is invested in the bank account advertised below. The bank pays compound interest.

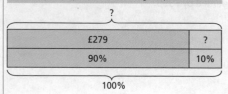

Collins Bank
4% interest paid annually for 5 years

Opening balance of £2000

a) How much will be in the account after 3 years?

A 4% increase means the new balance is 104% of the previous balance. The multiplier is 1.04. The value is increased by 4% each year.

New value in year 1:
£2000 × 1.04 = £2080
New value in year 2:
£2000 × 1.04 × 1.04 = £2163.20

New value in year 3:
£2000 × 1.04 × 1.04 × 1.04
= £2249.73

Each year, the previous balance is multiplied by 1.04. A faster way of writing this is £2000 × 1.04^x (where x is the number of years).

b) How much will be in the account after 5 years?

After 5 years,
£2000 × 1.04^5 = £2433.31

To quickly find a repeated percentage change:
New value = original value × multiplier^x (where x is the number of changes)

Finding the original value

Finding the original value of a percentage change involves using **reverse percentages**. Think about the calculation required to find the new value and use inverse operations to find the original value.

To find the original value, use the multiplier and inverse operations.

A games console is in a 10% off sale. Its new price is £279. Calculate the original price.

To find the multiplier, think about the percentage that the new price represents of the original price.

?		
£279		?
90%		10%
	100%	

The multiplier is 0.9

Say the original value is x. To find the sale price, the calculation would be $x \times 0.9 = £279$

$x \times 0.9 = £279$
$\div 0.9 \qquad \div 0.9$
$x = £310$

Use inverse operations: divide both sides by 0.9

The original price was £310.

Repeated percentage change and finding the original value

Percentage multipliers

1 Write down the multiplier for each of these percentage changes.

   a)   Increase by 56%   ....

   b)   Increase by 32%   ....

   c)   Decrease by 4%   ....

   d)   Decrease by 21%   ....

Repeated percentage change

2 A bank account pays compound interest of 3% a year.

If no additional deposits are made, find the balance after 5 years with a starting balance of £1200.

3 A car depreciates (goes down) in value by 8% each year.
The car costs £20 000 when new.

Calculate the value of the car after 10 years.

Finding the original value

4 A shop is having a sale of 10% off all mobile phones.
A mobile phone costs £180 in the sale.

What was the original price?

5 A computer store is increasing its prices by 8% on all items.
After the increase, a laptop costs £850.

What was the price before the increase?

5 Direct proportion

Direct proportion word problems

Two quantities are in **direct proportion** when they increase or decrease at the **same rate**.

Sam can type 80 words in 1 minute. How many words can Sam type in 10 minutes?

$\times 10$ (80 words = 1 minute) $\times 10$
800 words = 10 minutes

For every minute, Sam types 80 words. To work out how many words Sam will type in 10 minutes, you need 10 lots of 80.

Kelly works for 5 hours and gets paid £40. How much will Kelly be paid for working 6 hours?

$\div 5$ (5 hours = £40) $\div 5$
$\times 6$ (1 hour = £8) $\times 6$
6 hours = £48

For every hour that Kelly works, she will be paid the same amount. To find out how much Kelly gets paid for 1 hour of work, divide £40 by 5. This means that for every hour Kelly works, she gets paid £8.
To work out how much Kelly will get paid for working 6 hours, you need 6 lots of £8.

400 g of sugar is needed to bake a cake for 8 people. How much sugar is needed to bake a cake for 10 people?

$\div 4$ (400 g = 8 people) $\div 4$
$\times 5$ (100 g = 2 people) $\times 5$
500 g = 10 people

The **highest common factor** of 8 people and 10 people is 2 people. Therefore, to work out how many grams of sugar are needed for 10 people, find out how many grams of sugar are needed for 2 people, and multiply this by 5.

Direct proportion formula

To express that y is directly proportional to x, the α symbol is used. $y \, \alpha \, x$ means that y is directly proportional to x. This can be converted into the formula:

$$y = kx$$

k is a **constant**

A constant is a fixed number that does not change.

A is directly proportional to B and when $A = 30$, $B = 6$. Find the value of A when $B = 10$.

$A \, \alpha \, B$

$A = kB$

$30 = k \times 6$ To find k, substitute in the values that are given.

$\div 6 \quad \div 6$

$5 = k$

$A = 5 \times 10$

$A = 50$

S is directly proportional to T and when $S = 10$, $T = 50$. Find the value of S when $T = 60$.

$S \, \alpha \, T$

$S = kT$

$10 = k \times 50$ To find k, substitute in the values that are given.

$\div 50 \quad \div 50$

$0.2 = k$

$S = 0.2 \times 60$

$S = 12$

⑤ Direct proportion

Direct proportion word problems

1 If 3 pencils cost 75p, how much do 6 pencils cost?

2 If 4 lollipops cost 80p, how much do 2 lollipops cost?

3 Jeremiah can type 60 words in 1 minute.
How many words can Jeremiah type in 3 minutes?

4 An electrician works for 3 hours and gets paid £150.
How much will the electrician be paid for working for 5 hours?

5 If 2 pencils cost 44p, how much will 9 pencils cost?

6 A car travels 120 miles in 4 hours at a steady speed.
How far does the car travel in 7 hours?

Direct proportion formula

7 A is directly proportional to B and when $A = 24$, $B = 4$.
Find the value of A when B is 9.

8 X is directly proportional to Y and when $X = 35$, $Y = 7$.
Find the value of X when Y is 9.

9 P is directly proportional to Q and when $P = 60$, $Q = 120$.
Find the value of P when Q is 100.

5 Inverse proportion

Inverse proportion word problems

Two quantities are in **inverse proportion** when as one quantity increases, the other quantity decreases at the **same rate**.

It takes 10 hours for 10 people to decorate some cakes. How long would it take 5 people to decorate the same number of cakes?

$$\div 2 \left(\begin{array}{l} 10 \text{ people} = 10 \text{ hours} \\ 5 \text{ people} = 20 \text{ hours} \end{array} \right) \times 2$$

It takes half the number of people double the amount of time (20 hours) to decorate the same number of cakes.

There is enough food to feed 11 chickens for 4 days. How many days of food are there if there are 2 chickens?

$$\begin{array}{l} \div 11 \left(\begin{array}{l} 11 \text{ chickens} = 4 \text{ days} \\ 1 \text{ chicken} = 44 \text{ days} \\ \times 2 \end{array} \right. \begin{array}{l} \times 11 \\ \\ \div 2 \end{array} \\ \qquad \quad 2 \text{ chickens} = 22 \text{ days} \end{array}$$

The fewer chickens there are, the greater the number of days' worth of food there is. There are 22 days of food for 2 chickens.

It takes 12 hours for 5 people to paint a room. How many people would be needed if the room had to be painted in 10 hours?

$$\begin{array}{l} \div 6 \left(\begin{array}{l} 12 \text{ hours} = 5 \text{ people} \\ 2 \text{ hours} = 30 \text{ people} \\ 10 \text{ hours} = 6 \text{ people} \end{array} \right. \begin{array}{l} \times 6 \\ \\ \div 5 \end{array} \\ \times 5 \end{array}$$

The **highest common factor** of 12 hours and 10 hours is 2 hours. Therefore, to work out how many people will be needed for 10 hours, find out how many people are needed for 2 hours. Then work out how many people are needed for 10 hours.

6 people are needed to complete the job in 10 hours.

Inverse proportion formula

To express that y is inversely proportional to x, the α symbol is used. $y \alpha \frac{1}{x}$ means that y is inversely proportional to x. This can be converted into the formula:

$$y = \frac{k}{x}$$

k is a **constant**

A constant is a fixed number that does not change.

A is inversely proportional to B and when $A = 3$, $B = 9$. Find the value of A when $B = 3$.

$A \alpha \frac{1}{B}$

$A = \frac{k}{B}$

$3 = \frac{k}{9}$ To find k, substitute in the values that are given.

$\times 9 \quad \times 9$

$27 = k$

$A = \frac{27}{3}$

$A = 9$

P is inversely proportional to Q and when $P = 3$, $Q = 15$. Find the value of Q when $P = 5$.

$P \alpha \frac{1}{Q}$

$P = \frac{k}{Q}$

$3 = \frac{k}{15}$ To find k, substitute in the values that are given.

$\times 15 \quad \times 15$

$45 = k$

$5 = \frac{45}{Q}$

$\times Q \quad \times Q$

$5Q = 45$

$\div 5 \quad \div 5$

$Q = 9$

---

⑤ Inverse proportion

Inverse proportion word problems

1 It takes 10 people 20 hours to decorate some cakes.

How long would it take 5 people to decorate the same number of cakes?

....

2 It takes 4 builders 6 hours to build a wall.

How long would it take 12 builders to build the same wall?

....

3 It takes 4 teachers 8 hours to mark some exam papers.

How long would it take 1 teacher?

....

4 3 friends go camping and pack enough water to last for 6 days.

How long will the same amount of water last if 2 friends go camping?

....

5 It takes 2 people 5 hours to decorate some cakes.

How long would it take 5 people to decorate the same number of cakes?

....

6 4 people can paint a fence in 3 hours.

How long will it take 6 people to paint the fence?

....

Inverse proportion formula

7 A is inversely proportional to B and when $A = 4$, $B = 2$.

Find the value of A when B is 8.

....

8 X is inversely proportional to Y and when $X = 3$, $Y = 4$.

Find the value of X when Y is 2.

....

9 P is inversely proportional to Q and when $P = 4$, $Q = 5$.

Find the value of Q when P is 2.

....

Measures of central tendency and spread

Measures of central tendency

A measure of central tendency is a single value that attempts to describe a set of data by identifying its central position. **Mean, median** and **mode** are measures of central tendency:
- The mean is an **arithmetic average** found by adding together the values and dividing the total by the number of values in the data set.
- The median is the **middle value** when the data is ordered.
- The mode is the **most common** value in the data set.

The number of goals that were scored in 7 football matches are recorded. Find the mean number of goals scored.

1 3 4 6 6 7 8

To determine the mean, divide the total sum by the total number of items in the data set.

$1 + 3 + 4 + 6 + 6 + 7 + 8 = 35$
$35 \div 7 = 5$
The mean is 5 goals per game.

Find the median of this data set showing the number of goals scored in 7 football matches.

1 6 7 4 6 8 3

To find the median, put the numbers in **ascending** or **descending** order, and find the **middle value** by crossing out the numbers at each end of the data set.

1̶ 3̶ 4̶ 6 6̶ 7̶ 8̶

The median is 6 goals.

Find the median of the data set.

9 9 9 10 10 14 15 16 19 20

To find the median of a data set that has an even number of values, find the two middle numbers, add the two numbers together and divide the total by 2.

9̶ 9̶ 9̶ 10̶ 10 14 15̶ 16̶ 19̶ 20̶

$10 + 14 = 24$
$24 \div 2 = 12$
Median = 12

Find the mode of this data set showing the number of goals scored in 7 football matches.

1 3 4 6 6 7 8

To find the mode, look for the value that occurs the most often (i.e. the value that repeats more than any other value).

6 is the only value that is repeated in this data set.

The mode is 6 goals.

It is possible to have more than one mode or no mode at all.

Measuring the spread of data

The range measures the **spread** of the data set. To find the range, work out the difference between the highest and lowest values in the data set.

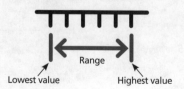

Lowest value   Highest value
Range

Find the range of this data set showing the number of goals scored in 7 football matches.

1 3 4 6 6 7 8

Range = highest value – lowest value
Range = 8 – 1
Range = 7 goals

Measures of central tendency and spread

Measures of central tendency

1 The number of hours that 5 students spent studying in one week was recorded as follows:

$$10 \quad 5 \quad 3 \quad 5 \quad 7$$

a) Work out the mean.

....

b) Work out the median.

....

c) Work out the mode.

....

2 The shoe sizes of 8 students were recorded as follows:

$$3 \quad 3 \quad 5 \quad 4 \quad 3 \quad 4 \quad 7 \quad 3$$

a) Work out the mean.

....

b) Work out the median.

....

c) Work out the mode.

....

Measuring the spread of data

3 The number of hours that 5 students spent studying in one week was recorded as follows:

$$10 \quad 5 \quad 1 \quad 5 \quad 7$$

Work out the range.

....

4 The shoe sizes of 8 students were recorded as follows:

$$3 \quad 3 \quad 5 \quad 4 \quad 3 \quad 4 \quad 7 \quad 3$$

Work out the range.

....

(6) Frequency tables

Data types and frequency tables

Data is a set of information that can be analysed. Data can be collected by using tables, which makes it easier to read and understand.

Qualitative data is data that describes something (e.g. colour of hair; colour of eyes).

Quantitative data is data that is numerical (e.g. height; shoe size).

There are two types of quantitative data:

- **Discrete** data can only take certain values (e.g. the number of people in a room; the number of pages in a book).
- **Continuous** data can take any value (e.g. the time taken to run a race; the mass of an object).

A **grouped** frequency table is used to organise and simplify a large set of data into smaller groups. A frequency table containing **ungrouped** data has data that has not been put into categories or simplified.

The heights of 16 students were recorded in centimetres. Organise the heights into a grouped frequency table.

| 159 | 140 | 145 | 149 | 150 | 134 | 144 | 151 |
| 155 | 144 | 157 | 141 | 158 | 146 | 132 | 160 |

Height, h cm	Frequency
$130 < h \leqslant 140$	3
$140 < h \leqslant 150$	7
$150 < h \leqslant 160$	6
	Total = 16

The line underneath the 'less than' symbols means 'less than or equal to'. Notice that a height of 140 cm is included in the first group.

The test scores of 21 students were recorded. Organise the test scores in an ungrouped frequency table.

| 6 | 10 | 10 | 9 | 7 | 8 | 7 | 9 | 9 | 5 | 6 | 8 | 7 |
| | | 9 | 8 | 10 | 9 | 7 | 9 | 10 | 5 | | | |

Test score	Tally	Frequency
5	||	2
6	||	2
7	||||	4
8	|||	3
9	|||| |	6
10	||||	4
		Total = 21

The **mean**, **median**, **mode** and **range** can be calculated from a frequency table.

$$\text{Mean} = \frac{\text{sum of all values}}{\text{number of values}}$$

$$= \frac{(5 \times 2) + (6 \times 2) + (7 \times 4) + (8 \times 3) + (9 \times 6) + (10 \times 4)}{21}$$

$$= 8$$

$$\text{Median} = \frac{21 + 1}{2} = \text{11th value}$$

$$= 8$$

The **mode** is the most common value. This is the test score with the highest frequency.

The **mode** is 9.

If the total frequency is odd, find the median by calculating $(n+1) \div 2$, where n is the number of values in the data set and the result is the position of the middle number.

$$\text{Range} = \text{highest score} - \text{lowest score}$$

$$= 10 - 5 = 5$$

Two-way frequency tables

A two-way frequency table is used to display data from two different categories.

Remember to include the totals for both categories in a two-way frequency table.

Primary and secondary students were asked if they eat breakfast in the mornings before school.
38 students in primary had breakfast. 12 students in primary did not have breakfast.
22 students in secondary had breakfast. 28 students in secondary did not have breakfast.
Record these results in a two-way frequency table.

	Breakfast	No breakfast	Total
Primary	38	12	50
Secondary	22	28	50
Total	60	40	100

Frequency tables

Data types and frequency tables

1) Here is a list of the colours of cars in a car park:

green, blue, green, red, red, green, yellow,
yellow, blue, red, green, yellow, yellow,
yellow, red, green, blue, red, red, yellow,
green, yellow, green, blue, yellow, blue,
blue, red, green, blue, yellow

Colour	Tally	Frequency
		Total =

a) Is this data quantitative or qualitative?

....

b) Display this data in a frequency table.

2) Here are the speeds of 20 vehicles, to the nearest mph:

45	65	72	48	74	67	68
46	56	53	58	68	72	64
62	49	72	55	67	51	

Complete the grouped frequency table.

Speed, x mph	Tally	Frequency
$40 < x \leqslant 50$		
$50 < x \leqslant 60$		
$60 < x \leqslant 70$		
$70 < x \leqslant 80$		

3) Here are the temperatures at midday for 7 days (in °C):

23, 24, 24, 23, 24, 25, 21

a) Display this data in an ungrouped frequency table.

b) What is the mean of this data? ....

c) What is the median of this data? ....

d) What is the mode of this data? ....

e) What is the range of this data? ....

Temperature	Tally	Frequency
21°C		
22°C		
23°C		
24°C		
25°C		

Two-way frequency tables

4) Students were asked what they ate for breakfast and lunch.

26 students who had porridge for breakfast had a sandwich for lunch.
14 students who had toast for breakfast had a sandwich for lunch.
10 students who had porridge for breakfast had a hot meal for lunch.
20 students who had toast for breakfast had a hot meal for lunch.

Complete the two-way frequency table.

	Sandwich	Hot meal	Total
Porridge			
Toast			
Total			

6 Bar charts and pictograms

Bar charts

A bar chart is used to display data using rectangular bars of different heights or lengths.

A bar chart must include:
- a title
- labels on both axes
- numbered frequency
- bars of equal width
- categories
- gaps of equal width between the bars.

This table shows the colours of cars that passed a school. Draw a bar chart for this information.

Colour	Frequency
Blue	5
Red	2
Green	8
Silver	1
Yellow	1
Black	2

Dual bar charts show a comparison between two or more sets of data.

Dual bar charts must include a key to identify the different categories.

This two-way frequency table shows the favourite sports of some adults and children. Draw a dual bar chart for this information.

	Football	Running	Swimming
Adults	4	5	3
Children	3	7	6

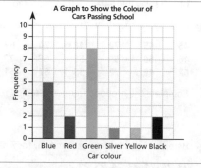

Pictograms

A pictogram can also represent data. Unlike a bar chart, a pictogram uses rows or columns of pictures to represent frequency.

Half a picture represents half of the frequency in the key.

The table below shows the favourite flavour of crisps of some students. Draw a pictogram for this information.

Crisp flavour	Frequency
Ready salted	28
Cheese and onion	16
Salt and vinegar	24
Chicken	10

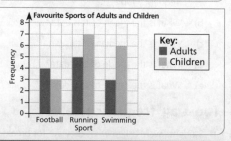

Bar charts and pictograms

Bar charts

1 The types of trees in a particular area were recorded in the frequency table.

Draw a bar chart to represent this information.

Tree	Frequency
Oak	2
Birch	5
Evergreen	8
Pine	10
Cedar	7

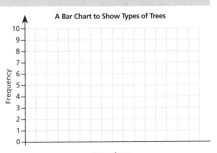

2 The eye colours of some boys and girls were recorded in the frequency table.

Draw a dual bar chart to represent this information.

Eye colour	Boys	Girls
Blue	8	7
Green	4	4
Brown	2	4

Pictograms

3 The table below shows the favourite sports of some Year 8 students.

Complete the pictogram to represent this information.

Sport	Frequency
Badminton	20
Netball	15
Basketball	25
Table tennis	5

Favourite Sports of Year 8 Students

Badminton	
Netball	
Basketball	
Table tennis	
Key:	= 5

4 The table below shows the number of cupcakes sold by a shop over 6 days.

Complete the pictogram to represent this information.

Day	Frequency
Monday	30
Tuesday	15
Wednesday	24
Thursday	21
Friday	42
Saturday	57

Number of Cupcakes Sold

Monday	
Tuesday	
Wednesday	
Thursday	
Friday	
Saturday	
Key:	= 6 cupcakes

Pie charts and scatter graphs

Pie charts

Pie charts use a circle to display data. Pie charts show the **proportion** or **fraction** of each category within the data compared to the whole circle.

To find the size of each angle, multiply the fraction by 360 because there are 360° in a circle. Always label the sections of a pie chart.

The frequency table (right) shows the favourite subject of 36 students. Draw a pie chart to show this data.

Subject	Frequency
Maths	12
English	10
Science	14

To find the size of each angle, express each subject's frequency as a fraction of the total number of students asked, and multiply this by 360°.

Subject	Frequency	Fraction	Angle
Maths	12	$\frac{12}{36}$	120°
English	10	$\frac{10}{36}$	100°
Science	14	$\frac{14}{36}$	140°

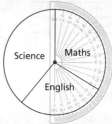

To draw a pie chart, use a **protractor** to mark off the angles that are needed.

You can find the frequency of a category if given the total frequency and the size of an angle in a pie chart.

The pie chart shows the proportion of different fish in a tank. There are 24 fish in total.

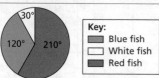

Key:
- Blue fish
- White fish
- Red fish

Work out how many blue fish are in the tank.

$\frac{120}{360} \times 24 = 8$

There are 8 blue fish in the tank.

Scatter graphs

Scatter graphs show the relationship between two sets of **numerical** data. The relationship is described using **correlation**. There are three types of correlation:

Correlation is strong if the points on a scatter graph closely follow a straight line. Correlation is weak if the points are more loosely spread from a straight line.

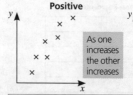

Positive — As one increases the other increases

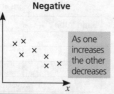

Negative — As one increases the other decreases

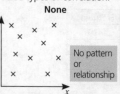

None — No pattern or relationship

A shopkeeper records the temperature for 8 days and the number of ice creams sold.

Temperature (°C)	Ice creams sold
20	14
15	10
25	16
10	6
20	15
5	2
15	12
12	10

a) Plot the data on a scatter graph.

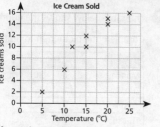

b) What type of correlation does the graph show?

A positive correlation. The higher the temperature, the more ice creams that are sold.

6 Pie charts and scatter graphs

Pie charts

1 The frequency table shows the favourite colour of 36 students.

Colour	Frequency	Fraction	Angle
White	9		
Green	20		
Red	7		

a) Complete the table.

b) Draw a pie chart to represent this information.

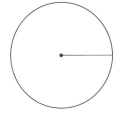

2 The pie chart shows the proportion of different fish in a tank. There are 48 fish in total.

a) Work out the number of blue fish in the tank. ....

b) Work out the number of white fish in the tank. ....

c) Work out the number of red fish in the tank. ....

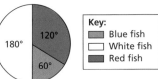

180° 120° 60°

Key:
- Blue fish
- White fish
- Red fish

Scatter graphs

3 The height and weight of 8 students are shown in the table.

a) Plot the data on a scatter graph.

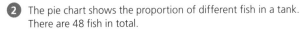

Weight and Height of 8 Students

Height (cm)	Weight (kg)
150	45
156	46
156	51
181	57
170	51
172	58
165	52
180	50

b) Describe the correlation between height and weight.

....

4 The number of hours spent on social media by people of different ages is shown in the table.

a) Plot the data on the scatter graph.

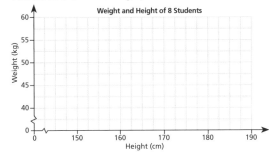

Hours Spent on Social Media per Day

Age	Hours spent on social media per day
10	10
15	8
21	6
27	4
32	2

b) Describe the correlation between age and the number of hours spent on social media in a day.

....

Interpreting statistical measures and representations

The bar chart shows information about the colour of cars passing a school over a 10-minute period.

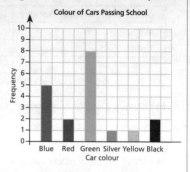

Colour of Cars Passing School

a) **How many blue cars drove past?**

   Read off the frequency from the y-axis of the blue car category.

   5 blue cars drove past.

b) **How many more green cars than silver cars drove past?**

   Find how many cars of each colour drove past and find the difference between them by **subtracting**.

   7 more green cars than silver cars drove past.

c) **What colour of car drove past the most?**

   Green cars had the highest frequency, so green cars drove past most often. This is the **mode**.

d) **How many cars drove past in total?**

   19 cars drove past in total. To find the total, add together the frequencies of each colour of car.

Choosing an appropriate statistical measure

When choosing an appropriate statistical measure, consider the advantages and disadvantages of each.

Measure of central tendency	Advantage	Disadvantage
Mean	Takes account of every value	Affected by very large or very small values
Median	Unaffected by very large or very small values	May not be an actual number in the data set
Mode	Only average that can be used for qualitative data	There may be more than one mode or no mode

The salaries of five employees in a company are:

£23 000 £25 000 £30 000 £33 000 £120 000

Which statistical measure should be used to represent the average?

The **median** should be used because it is unaffected by very large or very small values. £120 000 is a very large value compared to the others.

A shop wants to find the average size of shoe sold to help it to decide which size it needs most stock of. The sizes sold on a particular day are:

3, 4, 4, 5, 6, 7, 8, 8, 9, 9, 9, 9, 9, 10, 10, 11, 12, 14

Which statistical measure should be used for the average?

The **mode** (9) should be used because it shows which shoe size is in greatest demand.

The heights of some Year 8 students, in metres, are:

1.72, 1.54, 1.57, 1.50, 1.55, 1.46, 1.63, 1.61

Which statistical measure should be used for the average height?

The **mean** should be used because it takes account of every value and there are few very large or very small values in the data set.

> The range is not a measure of central tendency. It measures the spread of the data set.

The daily temperatures across March last year for two cities are summarised in this table.

City	Mean maximum daily temperature	Range of maximum daily temperature
A	22°C	6°C
B	22°C	13°C

Which city should you choose if you want to enjoy high temperatures? Justify your answer.

City A should be the city you choose to visit. Both cities have the same mean, but city A has the smaller range. This means that the temperature is more consistently high in city A compared to city B.

Interpreting statistical representations

Interpreting statistical measures and representations

1 The bar chart shows the preferred toast toppings of a group of students.

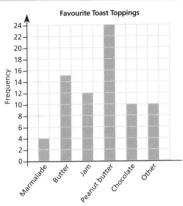

Favourite Toast Toppings

a) How many students prefer chocolate on their toast? ....

b) How many students prefer marmalade on their toast? ....

c) How many more students prefer butter on their toast than jam? ....

d) What is the mode of this data? ....

e) How many students took part in the survey? ....

Choosing an appropriate statistical measure

2 A boutique had daily sales of **£326, £540, £385, £450, £2435, £459** and **£493** over the last week.

Is the mean or median a more reliable measure of central tendency? Justify your answer.

....

....

3 The favourite subjects of some students were collected and recorded:

French, PE, Maths, Science, Maths, ICT, Maths, DT, Maths

Which measure of central tendency can best be used to describe this data? Justify your answer.

....

....

4 The daily temperatures across March last year for two cities are summarised in this table.

City	Mean maximum daily temperature	Range of maximum daily temperature
C	12°C	8°C
D	21°C	8°C

Which city should you choose to visit if you want to enjoy high temperatures? Justify your answer.

....

....

7 Properties of polygons

Properties of quadrilaterals

A **polygon** is a closed **2D shape** with sides that are straight lines. A **quadrilateral** is a polygon with:
* four sides
* four vertices
* interior angles that add up to 360°.

> A vertex is a corner. This is where two edges meet.

> Adjacent means 'next to'.

Rectangle	**Parallelogram**
All angles are **equal** (90°). Opposite sides are **equal** in length. Opposite sides are **parallel**.	Opposite angles are **equal**. Opposite sides are **parallel**. Opposite sides are **equal**. Diagonals **bisect** each other.
Square	**Rhombus**
All angles are **equal** (90°). All sides are **equal** in length. Opposite sides are **parallel**.	Opposite angles are **equal**. All sides are **equal** in length. Opposite sides are **parallel**.
Kite	**Trapezium**
Two pairs of **adjacent equal sides**. Opposite angles between the sides of different length are **equal**. Its long diagonal **bisects** the short diagonal at right angles.	One pair of **parallel** sides. The two angles at the end of each non-parallel side **add to 180°**.

Work out the size of the angle marked x in this quadrilateral.

To work out the size of x, add together the angles given and subtract from 360° because interior angles in a quadrilateral sum to 360°.

$88° + 91° + 66° = 245°$
$360° - 245° = 115°$
$x = 115°$

Properties of triangles

Triangles can be categorised by the length of their sides or by the size of their largest angle.

Categorised by side	**Categorised by angle**	Find the angle marked x in this triangle.
An **equilateral triangle** has three equal sides	An **acute triangle** has three angles < 90°	To work out the size of x, add together the angles given and subtract from 180° because interior angles in a triangle sum to 180°.
An **isosceles triangle** has two equal sides	A **right triangle** has one angle of 90°	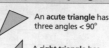
A **scalene triangle** has no equal sides	An **obtuse triangle** has one angle > 90°	$45° + 70° = 115°$ $180° - 115° = 65°$ $x = 65°$

7) Properties of polygons

Properties of quadrilaterals

1 Complete this table of the properties of quadrilaterals.

Quadrilateral	Image	Properties	
		Sides	Angles
Square		• Four equal sides • Opposite sides are parallel	
Rectangle			
			• Two opposite pairs of equal angles
Rhombus			• Two opposite pairs of equal angles
		• Two pairs of equal sides	• One opposite pair of equal angles
Trapezium			

2 Find the size of the angle marked x in this quadrilateral.

....

Properties of triangles

3 Complete this table of the properties of triangles.

Triangle	Equilateral triangle		Scalene triangle		Right triangle	Obtuse triangle
Image						
Properties		• Two sides are equal length • Two equal angles		• Has three angles that are all less than 90°	• Has one angle that	• Has one angle that ....

4 Find the size of the angle marked a in this triangle.

....

Solving problems with perimeter and area

Perimeter and area of triangles, parallelograms and trapeziums

Perimeter is the total distance around the outside of a **2D shape**. The perimeter is found by adding the side lengths together.

Area is the space inside a 2D shape.

Area of a triangle = $\dfrac{\text{base} \times \text{perpendicular height}}{2}$

Perpendicular height is the height that meets the base at a right angle. A right angle is 90°.

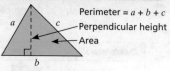
Perimeter = $a + b + c$
Perpendicular height
Area

Here is a triangle.
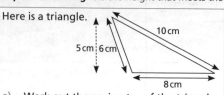

a) Work out the perimeter of the triangle.

Perimeter = 6 + 8 + 10 = 24 cm

b) Work out the area of the triangle.

Area = $\dfrac{8 \times 5}{2} = \dfrac{40}{2} = 20$ cm²

The area of this triangle is 25 cm². Find the perpendicular height, x.

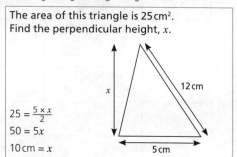

$25 = \dfrac{5 \times x}{2}$

$50 = 5x$

$10\,\text{cm} = x$

A **parallelogram** is a quadrilateral with two pairs of parallel sides.

Area of a parallelogram = length × width = base × perpendicular height

The area of a parallelogram is the same as the area of a rectangle, since you can form a parallelogram from a rectangle.

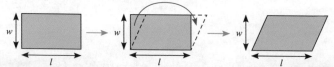

Calculate the area of this parallelogram.

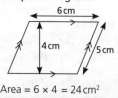

Area = 6 × 4 = 24 cm²

A **trapezium** is a quadrilateral with one pair of parallel sides.

Area of a trapezium = $\dfrac{(a + b)}{2} h$

where a and b are the parallel sides and h is the perpendicular height.

Work out the area of this trapezium.

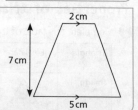

Area = $\dfrac{2 + 5}{2} \times 7$

= 3.5 × 7

= 24.5 cm²

Area of compound shapes

A compound shape is a 2D shape made up of two or more shapes joined together.

Work out the area of this compound shape.

Split the compound shape into smaller shapes (as done with the red dashed line).

Missing length of upper rectangle = 8 − 2 = 6 m

Area of upper rectangle = 6 × 3 = 18 m²   Find the areas of the smaller shapes.

Area of lower rectangle = 8 × 2 = 16 m²

Area of compound shape = 18 + 16 = 34 m²   Add the areas together.

Solving problems with perimeter and area

Perimeter and area of triangles, parallelograms and trapeziums

1 Here is a right-angled triangle.

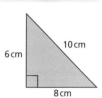

a) Work out its perimeter.

....

b) Work out its area.

....

2 Here is a scalene triangle.

Given that the area is 15 cm², work out the length marked by the arrow.

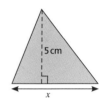

$x =$ ....

3 Here is a parallelogram.

a) Work out its perimeter.

....

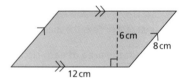

b) Work out its area.

....

4 Work out the perimeter of this trapezium.

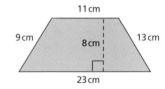

....

5 Work out the area of this trapezium.

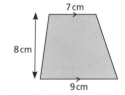

....

Area of compound shapes

6 Calculate the area of this compound shape.

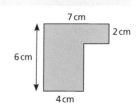

....

7 Area and circumference of a circle

Circumference of a circle

Circumference of a circle = perimeter of circle

Diameter = 2 × radius

$d = 2r$

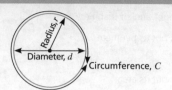

Circumference, C

Circumference of a circle: $C = 2\pi r$ or $C = \pi d$

Work out the circumference of each circle. Give your answers to 1 decimal place.

a)
5 cm

> You know the radius, so use $C = 2\pi r$

$C = 2\pi r$
$= 2 \times \pi \times 5$

> Use the π key on your calculator.

$= 31.41592...$
$C = 31.4\,\text{cm}$ (1 d.p.)

b)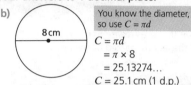
8 cm

> You know the diameter, so use $C = \pi d$

$C = \pi d$
$= \pi \times 8$
$= 25.13274...$
$C = 25.1\,\text{cm}$ (1 d.p.)

Area of a circle

The area of a circle is the space inside the circumference.

Area of a circle: $A = \pi r^2$

Work out the area of each circle. Give your answers to 1 decimal place.

a)
5 cm

$A = \pi r^2$
$= \pi \times 5^2$

> Use the π key on your calculator.

$= 78.5398...$
$A = 78.5\,\text{cm}^2$ (1 d.p.)

b)
8 cm

> You know the diameter, so find the radius first.

$r = 8 \div 2 = 4$
$A = \pi r^2$
$= \pi \times 4^2$
$= 50.2654...$
$A = 50.3\,\text{cm}^2$ (1 d.p.)

Area and circumference problems

Remember which formula is which.

Area

² in formula and units

$A = \pi r^2$ measured in cm² (or km² or m² or mm²)

Circumference

No ² in formula or units

$C = 2\pi r$ or $C = \pi d$ measured in cm
(or km or m or mm)

A circle has circumference 36 cm. Work out its area. Give your answer to 1 decimal place.

$2\pi r = 36$ Use $C = 2\pi r$ to write an equation.

$\div 2\pi \left(\begin{array}{c} 2\pi r = 36 \\ r = \dfrac{36}{2\pi} \end{array} \right) \div 2\pi$

> Solve the equation to find r.

$r = 5.7295...$ cm

> Use a calculator. Keep several decimal places in your value for r.

$A = \pi r^2$
$= \pi \times 5.7295^2$

> Use your value of r.

$= 103.1295...$
$A = 103.1\,\text{cm}^2$ (1 d.p.) Round to 1 decimal place.

7 Area and circumference of a circle

Circumference of a circle

1 Work out the circumference of each circle. Give your answers to 1 decimal place.

a)

12 cm

b)

7 cm

Area of a circle

2 Work out the area of each circle. Give your answers to 1 decimal place.

a)

12 cm

b)

7 cm

Area and circumference problems

3 A circle has circumference 50 cm.

Work out its radius. Give your answer to 1 decimal place.

4 A circle has circumference 72 cm.

Work out its diameter. Give your answer to 1 decimal place.

5 A circle has area 48 cm².

Giving your answers to 1 decimal place, work out:

a) its radius

b) its diameter

c) its circumference

Surface area of prisms

The surface area of a 3D shape is the total area of all the faces of the shape. To work out the surface area of a prism, sketch a net of the shape to identify the number of faces and their dimensions. You can then work out the areas and add them together to find the total surface area.

> A net is a 2D shape that can be folded up to make a 3D shape.

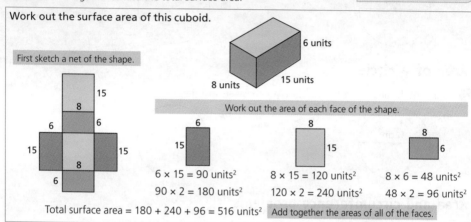

Work out the surface area of this cuboid.

First sketch a net of the shape.

Work out the area of each face of the shape.

$6 \times 15 = 90$ units^2
$90 \times 2 = 180$ units^2

$8 \times 15 = 120$ units^2
$120 \times 2 = 240$ units^2

$8 \times 6 = 48$ units^2
$48 \times 2 = 96$ units^2

Total surface area = 180 + 240 + 96 = 516 units^2 Add together the areas of all of the faces.

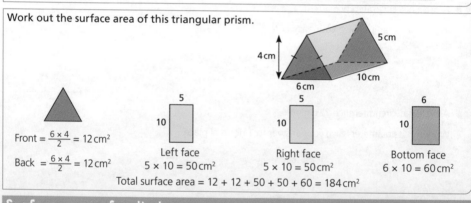

Work out the surface area of this triangular prism.

Front $= \dfrac{6 \times 4}{2} = 12$ cm^2

Back $= \dfrac{6 \times 4}{2} = 12$ cm^2

Left face
$5 \times 10 = 50$ cm^2

Right face
$5 \times 10 = 50$ cm^2

Bottom face
$6 \times 10 = 60$ cm^2

Total surface area = 12 + 12 + 50 + 50 + 60 = 184 cm^2

Surface area of cylinders

To work out the surface area of a cylinder, sketch a net of the cylinder.

You will need to work out the area of the two circles at the ends of the cylinder plus the area of the rectangle between them.

In a cylinder, the circumference of the circle is equal to the length of the rectangle.

Work out the surface area of this cylinder.

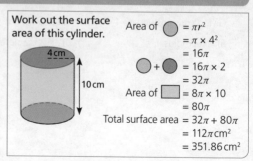

Area of ⬤ $= \pi r^2$
$= \pi \times 4^2$
$= 16\pi$

⬤ + ⬤ $= 16\pi \times 2$
$= 32\pi$

Area of ▭ $= 8\pi \times 10$
$= 80\pi$

Total surface area $= 32\pi + 80\pi$
$= 112\pi$ cm^2
$= 351.86$ cm^2

7 Surface area

Surface area of prisms

1 Work out the surface area of each cuboid.

a)

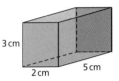

3 cm
2 cm
5 cm

b)

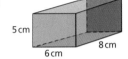

5 cm
6 cm
8 cm

2 Work out the surface area of each triangular prism.

a)

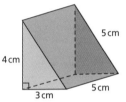

5 cm
4 cm
3 cm
5 cm

b)

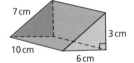

7 cm
3 cm
10 cm
6 cm

Surface area of cylinders

3 Work out the surface area of each cylinder.

a)

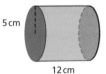

5 cm
12 cm

b)

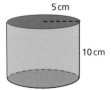

5 cm
10 cm

7 Solving problems with volume

Finding the unknown length of a prism

Volume is the space inside a 3D shape.

Volume = area of cross section × length

A **cross section** is the 2D shape that is seen when cutting through a 3D shape.

> The area of the cross section may not be given. If it is not given, calculate the area of the 2D cross section first, then find the unknown length.

Find the length of this cuboid given the volume and the area of the cross section.

Volume = 360 cm³

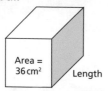

Length = $\frac{\text{volume}}{\text{area of cross section}}$

Length = $\frac{360}{36}$ = 10 cm

Find the height, h, of this cuboid given the width, length and volume.

Volume = 30 m³

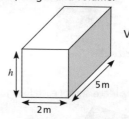

Area of the base = 2 × 5 = 10 m²

Height = 30 ÷ 10 = 3 m

Height = volume ÷ area of the base

Find the length, l, of this triangular prism given the base, perpendicular height and volume.

Volume = 40 cm³

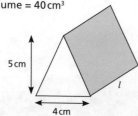

> In this example, the cross section is a triangular shape.

Volume = $\frac{1}{2}$ × base × perpendicular height × length

Length = $\frac{2 \times \text{volume}}{\text{base} \times \text{perpendicular height}}$

Length = $\frac{2 \times 40}{4 \times 5}$

Length = $\frac{80}{20}$ = 4 cm

Finding the unknown length of a cylinder

Find the height, h, of this cylinder given the volume and the cross-sectional area.

Volume = 72π m³

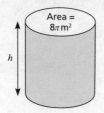

Height = $\frac{\text{volume}}{\text{area of cross section}}$

Height = $\frac{72\pi}{8\pi}$

Height = 9 m

7 Solving problems with volume

Finding the unknown length of a prism

1 Find the length, l, of each cuboid.

a) Volume = 80 cm³

Area = 10 cm² l

....

b) Volume = 45 cm³

Area = 9 cm² l

....

c) Volume = 600 cm³

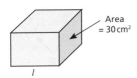

Area = 30 cm²

l

....

d) Volume = 36 m³

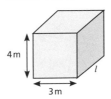

4 m

l

3 m

....

2 Find the height, h, of this cuboid.

Volume = 240 cm³

h

6 cm

4 cm

....

3 Find the length, l, of each triangular prism.

a) Volume = 30 cm³

3 cm

l

4 cm

....

b) Volume = 48 mm³

6 mm

l

4 mm

....

Finding the unknown length of a cylinder

4 Find the height, h, of each cylinder.

a) Volume = 54π m³

Area = 6π m²

h

....

b) Volume = 66π cm³

Area = 11π cm²

h

....

⑧ Angle properties

Angle facts

Acute angle	Right angle	Obtuse angle	Straight line	Reflex angle	Angles at a point	Vertically opposite
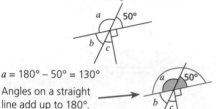						
Less than 90°	90°	Between 90° and 180°	180°	Between 180° and 360°	Angles at a point add up to 360°	Vertically opposite angles are equal

Find the sizes of the angles labelled with letters. Give reasons for your answers.

$b = 50°$

$a = 180° - 50° = 130°$

Angles on a straight line add up to 180°.

Vertically opposite angles are equal.

$c + 90° + 50° = 180°$
$c = 180° - 140° = 40°$

Angles on a straight line add up to 180°.

OR

Angles on a straight line add up to 180°.

Angles in triangles and quadrilaterals

Angles in a triangle add up to 180°.

Equilateral	Isosceles	Right-angled	Scalene
All angles are 60°	Two equal angles at the base of the equal sides	One angle of 90°	No equal angles

ABC is an isosceles triangle.
Work out the size of angle x.

Angle B = 70°

Base angles of an isosceles triangle are equal.

Angle $x = 180° - 70° - 70° = 40°$

Angles in a triangle add up to 180°.

The equal angles at the base of the equal sides in an isosceles triangle may not be at the bottom of the diagram.

Angles in a quadrilateral add up to 360°.

Rectangle or Square	Parallelogram or Rhombus	Isosceles trapezium	Kite
All angles are 90°	Opposite angles are equal	Two pairs of equal angles	One pair of equal angles

Angle properties

Angle facts

1 Work out the size of each angle labelled with a letter. Give reasons for your answers.

a)

25°
x

$x =$ ....

....

b)

40°
140°
v
w

$v =$ ....

$w =$ ....

c)

z
35°

$z =$ ....

....

d)

c
40°
b
a
60°

$a =$ ....

$b =$ ....

$c =$ ....

e)

3*n*
2*n*

$2n =$ ....

$3n =$ ....

Angles in triangles and quadrilaterals

2 Work out the size of each angle labelled with a letter. Give reasons for your answers.

a)

d
55°

$d =$ ....

....

b)
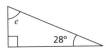
e
28°

$e =$ ....

....

c)
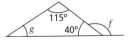
115°
g
40°
f

$f =$ ....

$g =$ ....

d)

80°
h

$h =$ ....

....

e)

i
j

$i =$ ....

$j =$ ....

f)

100°
m
50°
n

$m =$ ....

$n =$ ....

g)

100° *p*
q
r

$p =$ ....

$q =$ ....

$r =$ ....

h)

s
t
45°
u

$s =$ ....

$t =$ ....

$u =$ ....

⑧ Angles in parallel lines

Angles in parallel lines

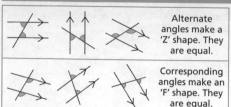

Alternate angles make a 'Z' shape. They are equal.

Corresponding angles make an 'F' shape. They are equal.

The 'F' and the 'Z' may be upside down or back to front.

You may also need to use these angle facts.

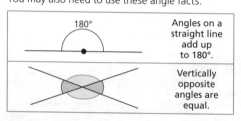

Angles on a straight line add up to 180°.

Vertically opposite angles are equal.

Find the sizes of the angles labelled with letters. Give reasons for your answers.

a)

Use 'F' and 'Z' to identify the angles, but write their proper names to give reasons.

$x = 110°$ Corresponding angles
$y = 180° - 110° = 70°$ Angles on a straight line add up to 180°

b)

Look for 'F' or 'Z' angles.

$u = 50°$ Alternate angles
$v = 180° - 50° = 130°$ Angles on a straight line add up to 180°

Solving parallel line problems

You may need to work out other angles before you can work out the value of the labelled angle. Parallel lines in an angle problem mean there will be alternate and corresponding angles.

Find the sizes of the angles labelled with letters. Give reasons for your answers.

a)

x and 100° are not alternate or corresponding angles. Draw in an angle that is either alternate or corresponding to 100°.

$y = 100°$ Alternate angles
$x = 180° - 100° = 80°$ Angles on a straight line add up to 180°

b)

a and 60° are not alternate or corresponding angles. Draw in an angle that is either alternate or corresponding to 60°.

$b = 60°$ Corresponding angles
$a = 60°$ Vertically opposite angles

Proving angle facts

A proof is a logical chain of reasoning to show a fact is true.

Use this diagram to prove that the angles in a triangle add up to 180°.

Draw and label angles that are alternate to a and c.

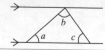

a, b and c make a straight line, so $a + b + c = 180°$
The angles in a triangle add up to 180°.

⑧ Angles in parallel lines

Angles in parallel lines

① Work out the size of each angle labelled with a letter. Give reasons for your answers.

a)

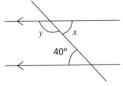

$x =$ ....

....

$y =$ ....

....

b)

$a =$ ....

....

$b =$ ....

....

Solving parallel line problems

② Work out the size of each angle labelled with a letter. Give reasons for your answers.

a)

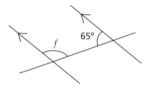

$f =$ ....

....

b)

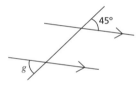

$g =$ ....

....

Proving angle facts

③ This diagram shows two pairs of parallel lines that cross to make a parallelogram.

Use the diagram to prove that opposite angles in a parallelogram are equal.

Label equal angles with the same letter.

....

....

8 Angles in polygons

Interior and exterior angles

A polygon is a shape with straight sides.
A polygon has interior and exterior angles.

Exterior angle + interior angle = 180°

The exterior angles of any polygon add up to 360°.

Interior angle

Exterior angle

Exterior angle
+ interior angle
= 180° because
angles on a
straight line add
up to 180°

Find the angles labelled with letters in this irregular pentagon.

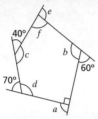

$a = 180° - 90° = 90°$

$b = 180° - 60° = 120°$

$c = 180° - 40° = 140°$

$d = 180° - 70° = 110°$

$e = 360° - 60° - 90° - 70° - 40° = 100°$

The exterior angles of a polygon add up to 360°.

$f = 180° - 100° = 80°$

Use angles on a
straight line to find
angles a to d and f.

Angles in regular polygons

In a regular polygon:

- all interior angles are equal
- all exterior angles are equal
- exterior angle $= \frac{360}{n}$ where n = number of sides.

a) Find the size of an exterior angle of a regular nonagon.

A regular nonagon has 9 sides and 9 equal exterior angles.

Exterior angle of regular nonagon $= \frac{360°}{9} = 40°$

b) Find the size of one of its interior angles.

Interior angle
$= 180° -$ exterior angle
$= 180° - 40° = 140°$

Exterior angle + interior angle = 180°

The diagram shows one interior and one exterior angle of a regular polygon.

How many sides does this polygon have?

156°

Exterior angle $= 180° - 156° = 24°$

$24° \times$ number of exterior angles $= 360°$

Exterior angles of a polygon add up to 360°.

Number of exterior angles $= \frac{360}{24} = 15$

The polygon has 15 sides.

Angle sum of a polygon

The angle sum of a polygon is the sum of its interior angles.

Triangle	Quadrilateral	Pentagon	Hexagon
Angle sum = 180°	Angle sum = 2 × 180° = 360°	Angle sum = 3 × 180° = 540°	Angle sum = 4 × 180° = 720°

Angle sum = (number of sides − 2) × 180°

$= (n - 2) × 180°$ n = number of sides

Find the angle sum of a 10-sided polygon.

$(n - 2) × 180°$ Substitute $n = 10$.

$= (10 - 2) × 180° = 8 × 180° = 1440°$

⑧ Angles in polygons

Interior and exterior angles

① Work out the size of each angle labelled with a letter.

a)

$a =$ ....

$b =$ ....

$c =$ ....

$d =$ ....

$e =$ ....

b)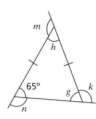

$g =$ ....

$h =$ ....

$k =$ ....

$m =$ ....

$n =$ ....

Angles in regular polygons

② Find the size of an exterior angle and an interior angle of a regular octagon.

Exterior angle = ...   Interior angle = ...

③ The diagram shows one interior and one exterior angle of a regular polygon. The interior angle is 150°.

How many sides does this polygon have?   ....

Angle sum of a polygon

④ Find the angle sum of a seven-sided polygon.

....

⑤ The diagram shows a square and a regular hexagon.

Work out the size of angle x. $x =$ ....

⑥ The diagram shows an equilateral triangle and a regular pentagon.

Work out the size of angle y. $y =$ ....

Drawing triangles accurately

You can draw triangles accurately using a ruler and a protractor.

Draw these triangles accurately. | Use a sharp pencil. Measure lines and angles carefully.

a)

1. Draw a base line 5 cm long and draw a 60° angle at the left-hand end.

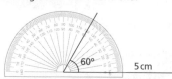

2. Draw a 45° angle at the right-hand end. Draw the two sides long enough to cross.

Don't rub out the extra lines.

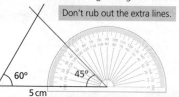

b)

1. Draw a base line 5 cm long and draw a 50° angle at the left-hand end.

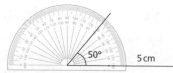

2. Draw the angle line 5 cm long. Then join the ends of the two lines using a ruler.

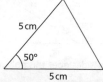

Constructing a triangle

'Construct' means 'draw accurately using a ruler and a pair of compasses'. You can construct a triangle when you know the lengths of all three sides.

Construction of a triangle of sides 4 cm (base), 5 cm and 6 cm

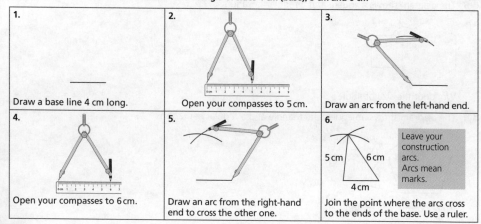

1.	2.	3.
Draw a base line 4 cm long.	Open your compasses to 5 cm.	Draw an arc from the left-hand end.
4.	5.	6.
Open your compasses to 6 cm.	Draw an arc from the right-hand end to cross the other one.	Join the point where the arcs cross to the ends of the base. Use a ruler.

6. Leave your construction arcs. Arcs mean marks.

5 cm 6 cm

4 cm

⑨ Using triangles in constructions

Drawing triangles accurately

1 Draw these triangles accurately on plain paper, using a protractor and a ruler.

a)
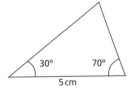

b)
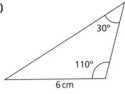

c)
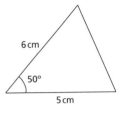

Constructing a triangle

2 Construct these triangles accurately on plain paper, using a ruler and pair of compasses.

a)

b)
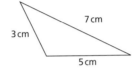

3 Construct an equilateral triangle with side length 6 cm, on plain paper.

Draw a sketch first.

4 Construct an isosceles triangle with side lengths 5 cm, 5 cm and 3.5 cm, on plain paper.

5 Construct this rhombus accurately on plain paper.

Construct two congruent isosceles triangles from the same base line.

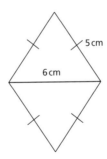

Perpendicular bisector and perpendicular line through a point

Perpendicular bisector

Bisect means 'cut in half'. 'Construct' means 'draw accurately using a ruler and a pair of compasses'.

> A perpendicular bisector cuts a line in half, at right angles.

Construct the perpendicular bisector of the line AB.

A ——————————————— B

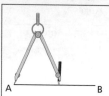	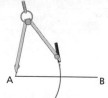	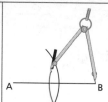	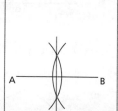
Put the compass point on point A. Open the compasses to just over halfway along the line. Use a sharp pencil.	Draw an arc. Keep the compasses open the same distance for the whole construction.	Move the compass point to B. Draw an arc.	Use a ruler to draw a straight line joining the two points where the arcs cross. Don't rub out the arcs!

Perpendicular line through a point on a line

Construct a line through point P that is perpendicular to the line AB.

A ——————•———— B
　　　　　　P

Put the compass point on point P.

Draw an arc that cuts the line AB twice.

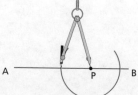

Construct the perpendicular bisector of the line between the two points where the first arc cuts.

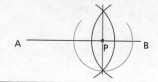

Perpendicular line through a point to a line

Draw a perpendicular line through point M to the line AB.

•M

A ——————————— B

Put your compass point on point M.

Draw an arc that cuts the line AB twice.

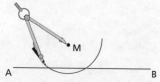

Construct the perpendicular bisector of the line between the two points where the first arc cuts.

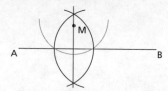

Perpendicular bisector

1 Construct the perpendicular bisector of each line. | Turn around the page if it helps. |

a)

A ——————— B

b)

P
|
|
|
|
Q

Perpendicular line through a point on a line

2 **a)** Construct a line through point C and perpendicular to the line AB.

A ——•—— B
    C

b) Construct a line through point D and perpendicular to the line PQ.

P
|
D•|
|
Q

3 Construct a 90° angle at point X.

| Use only pencil, ruler and compasses. Extend the line XY beyond X to draw your first arc. |

X•——————————— Y

Perpendicular line through a point to a line

4 **a)** Construct a line through point E and perpendicular to the line AB.

• E

A ——————— B

b) Construct a line through point F and perpendicular to the line PQ.

F
•

P
|
|
|
Q

⑨ Angle bisectors

Constructing an angle bisector

An angle bisector cuts an angle in half.

Construct the angle bisector of this angle.

Use a sharp pencil and keep the compasses open the same distance for the whole construction.

Put the compass point on the angle.

Open the compasses to just over halfway along the line. Draw an arc.

Move the compass point to where the arc crosses a line.

Draw an arc.

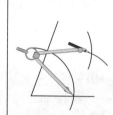

Move the compass point to where the arc crosses the other line.

Draw an arc.

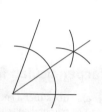

Use a ruler to draw the angle bisector.

Don't rub out the construction arcs. Arcs mean marks.

Constructing accurate angles

Construct a 45° angle.

Construct the perpendicular bisector of a line (see page 70).

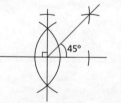

Bisect one of the 90° angles.

Construct a 30° angle.

Use compasses to construct an equilateral triangle.

Bisect one of the 60° angles.

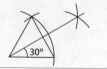

Constructing a rhombus

Construct this rhombus.

A rhombus has four equal sides.

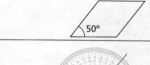

Use a protractor to draw a 50° angle.

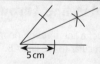

Open compasses to 5 cm.

Construct the angle bisector.

The diagonals of a rhombus bisect the angles.

Draw the other sides.

Angle bisectors

Constructing an angle bisector

1 Construct the angle bisector of this angle.

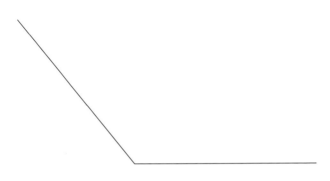

Constructing accurate angles

2 Construct an accurate 45° angle on this line.

Constructing a rhombus

3 Construct an accurate 60° angle.

Construct an equilateral triangle.

Use your 60° angle to construct this rhombus accurately.

4 cm

60°

Mixed questions

1 Round each number to 3 significant figures.

   a)   12 567

   b)   1.018 375

   c)   0.009 183

2 Complete the table.

Fraction	Decimal	Percentage
$\frac{2}{5}$		
	0.45	
		75%
	0.875	

3 The number of students absent from a year group over 10 days was as follows:

3   2   0   0   1   1   0   2   3   4

   a)   Work out the mean.

   b)   Work out the mode.

   c)   Work out the median.

   d)   Work out the range.

4 This list shows how some students travel to school.

walk, bus, bike, walk, bike, bus, walk, car, walk, bike, bike, bus, walk, walk, walk, car, bus, walk, bus, bus, walk, car, car, walk, walk, train, bike, bus, walk, walk

Transport	Tally	Frequency
		Total =

   a)   Is this data quantitative or qualitative?

   b)   Display this data in a frequency table.

5 Here is a sequence: 2, 8, 14, 20, 26 …

   a)   Is the sequence arithmetic or geometric?

   b)   Find the nth term rule for the sequence.

6 Here are the coordinates of some points: $(-3, -9)$ $(0, -3)$ $(1, -1)$ $(3, 3)$

   On which of the following lines do **all** the points lie? Circle your answer.

   $y = 3x$ $y = x - 3$ $y = x$ $y = 2x - 3$

Mixed questions

7 Find the equations of these lines.

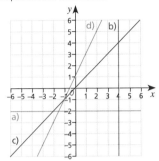

a) ....

b) ....

c) ....

d) ....

8 Solve each of the following equations.

a) $4x - 7 = 17$

b) $10x + 3 = 8$

$x = $ ....

$x = $ ....

c) $\frac{x}{3} + 5 = 9$

d) $\frac{x+5}{3} = 9$

$x = $ ....

$x = $ ....

9 A local sports event attracted 4500 spectators.
This was an increase of 6% on last year.

How many spectators attended last year? ....

10 Use the pictogram to answer the following questions.

Pizzas Sold

Cheese and tomato	●●●●
Mixed vegetable	●●◖
Ham and pineapple	●◖
Pepperoni	●●●
Barbecue chicken	●●●●◢

Key: ● = 4 pizzas

a) How many pizzas were sold in total? ....

b) Which pizza was least popular? ....

c) What is the difference between the number of barbecue chicken pizzas sold
and the number of mixed vegetable pizzas sold?

....

Mixed questions

11 Expand and simplify the following expression.

$5(x + 3) - 2(2x - 1)$

....

12 18 people were asked to answer 'yes' or 'no' as to whether they like cheese. The results are shown in the frequency table.

Answer	Frequency	Fraction	Angle
Yes	16		
No	2		

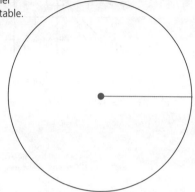

a) Complete the table to prepare a pie chart.

b) Draw a pie chart to represent this information.

13 Solve each of the following equations.

a) $7x + 9 = 2x - 6$

b) $2x - 1 = 6 - 5x$

$x = $ ....

$x = $ ....

14 In each case, find the new value.

a) A jacket priced at £64.99, now with 15% off

....

b) A car that cost £24 000 new but has now depreciated in value by 20%

....

c) An antique vase that has increased in value by 8% since being bought for £375

....

15 The area of the rectangle shown is 24 cm².

Use the information given to form an equation and solve it to find x.

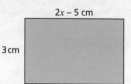

2x – 5 cm

3 cm

$x = $ ....

Mixed questions

16 Which of the following lines is parallel to the line with equation $y = \frac{1}{2}x + 5$? Circle your answer.

$2x + y = 10$ $2y - x + 6 = 0$ $y = 5 - 2x$ $2y + x = 1$

17 A house valued at £225 000 is expected to increase in value by 3% each year.

What is the expected value in 3 years' time?
Give your answer to the nearest thousand.

....

18 A running track has a perimeter of 400 metres.

What is the diameter, d, of the semi-circular ends?
Give your answer correct to the nearest metre.

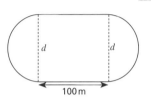

100 m

$d =$ ....

19 Give your answers to these correct to 1 decimal place.

a) Work out the surface area of a cylinder with radius 6 cm and height 12 cm.

.... cm²

b) Work out the height of a cylinder with diameter 11 cm and volume 2000 cm³.

.... cm

20 **a)** Y is directly proportional to X.

When $X = 8$, $Y = 36$.

Find Y when $X = 12$.

$Y =$ ....

b) B is inversely proportional to A.

When $A = 6$, $B = 8$.

Find B when $A = 16$.

$B =$ ....

Key facts and vocabulary

Number

Error interval	The true value can be up to half a unit either side of the measurement $166.5 \leqslant \text{length} < 167.5 \text{ cm}$
Percentage change	Percentage change $= \dfrac{\text{amount of increase or decrease}}{\text{original value}} \times 100$ Repeated percentage change: New value = original value $\times$ multiplier^x (where x is the number of changes)
Percentage increase and decrease	To increase a value by 20%, multiply by the multiplier $\dfrac{100 + 20}{100} = \dfrac{120}{100} = 1.2$ To decrease a value by 30%, multiply by the multiplier $\dfrac{100 - 30}{100} = \dfrac{70}{100} = 0.7$ To find the original value, use the multiplier and inverse operations
Rounding to significant figures	4852 rounded to 1 s.f. is 5000 0.00649 rounded to 1 s.f. is 0.006 4852 rounded to 2 s.f. is 4900 0.00649 rounded to 2 s.f. is 0.0065

Algebra

Arithmetic sequence	Terms go up or down by the same amount (common difference) each time 2, 5, 8, 11, 14, … Common difference +3 5, 3, 1, –1, –3, … Common difference –2
Direct proportion	As one quantity increases, the other quantity increases $y = kx$ at the same rate, e.g. when x doubles, y doubles k is a constant (a number that does not change)
Equation of a straight line	$y = mx + c$ where m is the gradient and c is the y-intercept
Expand	Multiply every term inside the bracket by the term outside the bracket $3(x + 4) = 3x + 12$ $5(2y - 1) = 10y - 5$
Geometric sequence	Each term is multiplied or divided by the same number to get the next term 2, 4, 8, 16, 32, … Each term is multiplied by 2 1000, 100, 10, 1, 0.1, … Each term is divided by 10
Gradient	Measure of the steepness of a line Positive gradient Negative gradient Gradient = 0 Gradient $= \dfrac{\text{change in } y}{\text{change in } x}$
Inverse proportion	As one quantity increases, the other quantity decreases $y = \dfrac{k}{x}$ at the same rate, e.g. when x doubles, y halves k is a constant

n^{th} term	Formula involving n that generates the terms in a sequence; substitute $n = 1$ to find the 1st term, $n = 2$ to find the 2nd term, and so on

$$\overset{\text{Common difference}}{\downarrow}$$
$$n^{th} \text{ term} = 2n + 1$$
$$\underset{\uparrow}{\phantom{n^{th} \text{ term} = 2n + 1}}$$
The constant

Geometry

Angle bisector	Cuts an angle in half
Angle facts	

Angles at a point	Vertically opposite	Equilateral triangle	Isosceles triangle
Angles at a point add up to 360°	Vertically opposite angles are equal	All angles are 60°	Two equal angles at base of equal sides

Angle sum	Angles in: • a triangle sum to 180° • a quadrilateral sum to 360° • an n-sided polygon sum to $(n - 2) \times 180°$
Angles in parallel lines	Alternate angles make a 'Z' shape; they are equal Corresponding angles make an 'F' shape; they are equal
Exterior angles	Interior angle Exterior angle Exterior angle + interior angle = 180° because angles on a straight line add up to 180°
Perpendicular bisector	Cuts a line in half, at right angles
Surface area	Total area of all faces of a 3D shape
Volume of a prism	Volume of prism = area of cross section × length Cross section Length

Statistics

Correlation	Positive (as one variable increases, the other increases) Negative (as one variable increases, the other decreases) None (no pattern or relationship)
Mean	$\dfrac{\text{Total sum of values}}{\text{Number of values}}$
Median	Middle value when values are in order In a set of n values, the median is the $\frac{n+1}{2}$th value
Mode	Most common value; the value with highest frequency
Range	Highest value – lowest value

Answers

Page 5: Significant figures

1. 68<u>1</u>24   94<u>3</u>9   70<u>6</u>23

   0.0057<u>3</u>   0.94<u>0</u>6   0.10<u>9</u>04

2.

	1 s.f.	2 s.f.	3 s.f.
57 271	60 000	57 000	57 300
843 913 759	800 000 000	840 000 000	844 000 000
83	80	83	83.0
1095	1000	1100	1100
165 878	200 000	170 000	166 000
2 475 000	2 000 000	2 500 000	2 480 000

3.

	1 s.f.	2 s.f.	3 s.f.
0.23696	0.2	0.24	0.237
0.059 218	0.06	0.059	0.0592
1.056	1	1.1	1.06
0.008	0.008	0.0080	0.00800
9.976	10	10	9.98
52.601	50	53	52.6

Page 7: Estimating calculations by rounding and limits of accuracy

1. a) i) $108.3 \div 6.24 \approx 100 \div 6 = \frac{50}{3} = 16\frac{2}{3}$

   ii) Underestimate (as 108.3 is rounded down quite a bit)

   b) i) $108.3 \div 6.24 \approx 108 \div 6 = 18$

   ii) Overestimate (as the divisor is rounded down and the dividend is not rounded by much)

   c) $108.3 \div 6.24 = 17.355769...$

2. a) i) $(2 \times £4) + £3 + (3 \times £3)$

   $= £8 + £3 + £9 = £20$

   ii) Underestimate (as the tea price is rounded down by more than the other prices are rounded up)

   b) $(2 \times £3.97) + £2.95 + (3 \times £3.17) = £20.40$

3. a) $31.5\,cm \leqslant$ height of jug $< 32.5\,cm$

   b) $106.5\,ml \leqslant$ volume of milk $< 107.5\,ml$

   c) $5263.5\,km \leqslant$ distance from London to Boston $< 5264.5\,km$

Page 9: Introducing sequences

1. a) Geometric; the sequence is multiplying by 5

   b) Arithmetic; the sequence is decreasing by 5

   c) Arithmetic; the sequence is increasing by 2

   d) Geometric; the sequence is dividing by 2

2. a) First term 7; common difference +5

   b) First term 11; common difference −4

3. a) 77, 70, 63, 56, 49

   b) −6, −3, 0, 3, 6

4. a) First term 3; multiply by 3

   b) First term 54; divide by 3

5. −1, −3, −9, −27, −81

Page 11: n^{th} term rules

1. a) 1st term $n = 1$ $(4 \times 1) + 9 = 13$

   2nd term $n = 2$ $(4 \times 2) + 9 = 17$

   3rd term $n = 3$ $(4 \times 3) + 9 = 21$

   10th term $n = 10$ $(4 \times 10) + 9 = 49$

   b) 1st term $n = 1$ $(2 \times 1) - 5 = -3$

   2nd term $n = 2$ $(2 \times 2) - 5 = -1$

   3rd term $n = 3$ $(2 \times 3) - 5 = 1$

   10th term $n = 10$ $(2 \times 10) - 5 = 15$

2. a) 1st term $n = 1$ $1^2 + 5 = 6$

   2nd term $n = 2$ $2^2 + 5 = 9$

   3rd term $n = 3$ $3^2 + 5 = 14$

   10th term $n = 10$ $10^2 + 5 = 105$

   b) 1st term $n = 1$ $1^3 - 1 = 0$

   2nd term $n = 2$ $2^3 - 1 = 7$

   3rd term $n = 3$ $3^3 - 1 = 26$

   10th term $n = 10$ $10^3 - 1 = 999$

3. a) 1, 5, 9, 13, 17

   $+4 \ +4 \ +4 \ +4$

   1st term − Common difference

   $1 - 4 = -3$

   n^{th} term rule $= 4n - 3$

   b) 22, 17, 12, 7, 2

   $-5 \ -5 \ -5 \ -5$

   1st term − Common difference

   $22 - (-5) = 27$

   n^{th} term rule $= -5n + 27$

Page 13: Coordinates

1. a) A(−2, −5) B(−5, 4) C(6, 3) D(2, −3)

   b) i)

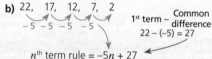

   ii) Trapezium

2. a) $y = x + 2$

b)

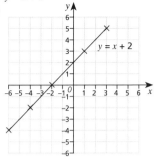

3. $y = 2x$

4. $y = x - 2$

5. $y = -3x$

Page 15: Gradient

1. a) 2   **b)** −3   **c)** $\frac{2}{3}$ **d)** $-\frac{1}{2}$

2.

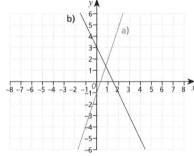

3. a) AB gradient 1; BC gradient −1

b)

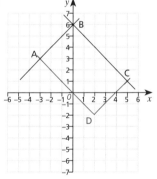

(2, −2)

Page 17: Graphing linear equations

1.

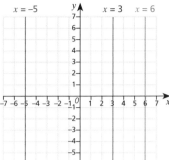

2.

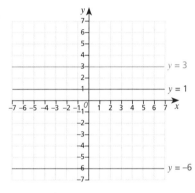

3.

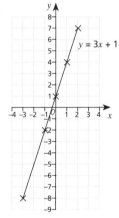

4.

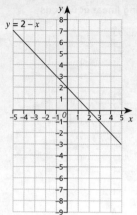

$y = 2 - x$

Page 19: $y = mx + c$

1. a) i) $y = \frac{1}{2}x + \frac{1}{4}$ **ii)** $y = -2x + 4$
   iii) $y = 2x + 3$
   b) $y = 2x + 3$

2. $5y + 2x = 4$ and $5y = 3 - 2x$

3.

Equation	Gradient	Coordinates of y-intercept
$y = 3x + 5$	3	(0, 5)
$y = -2x - 1$	-2	(0, -1)
$y = 6x$	6	(0, 0)
$y = -3$	0	(0, -3)
$y = 2 - x$	-1	(0, 2)
$2y = x - 7$	$\frac{1}{2}$ or 0.5	(0, -3.5)

4. $y = -x + 2$ and $y - 3x - 2 = 0$

5.

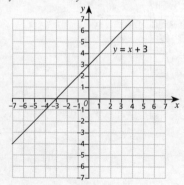

$y = x + 3$

6.

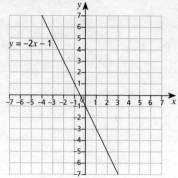

$y = -2x - 1$

Page 21: Linear relationships

1. a) Lie on straight line $y = 2x$
   b) Lie on straight line $y = x + 5$
   c) Do not lie on straight line

2. $y = 2(x - 1)$

3. a) $y = -x - 2$ **b)** $y = 3$
   c) $y = x + 3$ **d)** $x = 2$
   e) $y = 2x - 5$

4. $c = 2t + 10$ or $c = 2(t + 5)$

Page 23: Solving one-step equations

1. a)

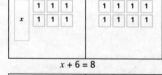

b)

2.

$x + 6 = 8$

Subtract 6 from both sides
$x + 6 - 6 = 8 - 6$

Simplify

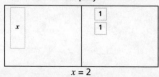

$x = 2$

3. a) $x = 6$ **b)** $x = 15$ **c)** $x = 8$

Page 25: Solving two-step equations

1.

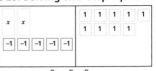

$$2x - 5 = 9$$

Add 5 to both sides
$$2x - 5 + 5 = 9 + 5$$

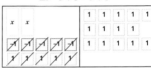

Simplify

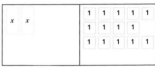

$$2x = 14$$

$$2x \div 2 = 14 \div 2$$

$$x = 7$$

2. a) $6x + 10 = 28$
$$6x = 18$$
$$x = 3$$

b) $\frac{x}{2} + 3 = 6$
$$\frac{x}{2} = 3$$
$$\frac{x}{2} \times 2 = 3 \times 2$$
$$x = 6$$

c) $5x - 4 = 41$
$$5x = 45$$
$$x = 9$$

d) $\frac{x}{6} + 8 = 14$
$$\frac{x}{6} = 6$$
$$x = 36$$

Page 27: Solving equations with variables on both sides

1. a)

$$x = 2$$

b)

$$b = 4$$

2.

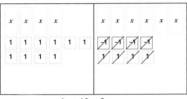

$$4x + 6 = 6x - 4$$

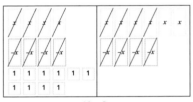

$$4x + 10 = 6x$$

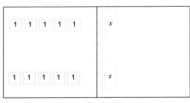

$$10 = 2x$$

$$5 = x$$

3. a) $2x + 6 = 5x - 15$
$$6 = 3x - 15$$
$$21 = 3x$$
$$7 = x$$

b) $3x - 4 = 20 - x$
$$3x = 24 - x$$
$$4x = 24$$
$$x = 6$$

Page 29: Solving equations with brackets

1. **a)** $3(2k - 4) + 5k = (3 \times 2k) + (3 \times -4) + 5k$
   $= 6k - 12 + 5k = 11k - 12$

   b) $k(2m - 4) = (k \times 2m) + (k \times -4) = 2km - 4k$

   c) $4(2x + 3y - 5) = (4 \times 2x) + (4 \times 3y) + (4 \times -5)$
   $= 8x + 12y - 20$

2. **a)** $3(k - 5) = 12$
   $k - 5 = 4$
   $k = 9$

   b) $2x + 3(4 - x) = 10$
   $2x + 12 - 3x = 10$
   $12 - x = 10$
   $12 = 10 + x$
   $2 = x$, so $x = 2$

3. **a)** $2(x + 3) + 4(x - 5) = 10$
   $2x + 6 + 4x - 20 = 10$
   $6x - 14 = 10$
   $6x = 24$
   $x = 4$

   b) $5(y - 2) = 3(y - 2) + 2$
   $5y - 10 = 3y - 6 + 2$
   $5y - 10 = 3y - 4$
   $5y = 3y + 6$
   $2y = 6$
   $y = 3$

Page 31: Multiplicative relationships

1. **a)** $\frac{12}{5}$ **b)** $\frac{7}{8}$ **c)** 2 **d)** $\frac{8}{10}$
2. A and D
3. **a)** $300 \times 1.47 = \$441.00$
   b) $75 \div 1.47 = £51.02$
4. $36 \div \frac{8}{5} = 22.5$ miles

Page 33: Percentages

1.

Fraction	$\frac{19}{50}$	$\frac{37}{50}$	$\frac{13}{100}$
Decimal	0.38	0.74	0.13
%	38%	74%	13%
Diagram			

2. **a)** $\frac{2}{18} = 2 \div 18 = 0.\dot{1}$
   $0.\dot{1} \times 100 = 11.\dot{1} = 11\%$ (to the nearest percent)

   b) $\frac{5}{38} = 5 \div 38 = 0.13157...$
   $0.13 \times 100 = 13\%$ (to the nearest percent)

3. 1 adult and 3 children tickets cost
   $£40 + (3 \times £19) = £97$
   $8\% = 8 \div 100 = 0.08$
   $0.08 \times £97 = £7.76$

Page 35: Percentage changes

1. **a)** $100\% - 15\% = 85\%$
   $85\% = 85 \div 100 = 0.85$
   $£850 \times 0.85 = £722.50$

   b) $100\% - 5\% = 95\%$
   $95\% = 95 \div 100 = 0.95$
   $£445 \times 0.95 = £422.75$

2. **a)** $100\% + 8\% = 108\%$
   $108\% = 108 \div 100 = 1.08$
   $475 g \times 1.08 = 513 g$

   b) $100\% + 20\% = 120\%$
   $120\% = 120 \div 100 = 1.2$
   $910 g \times 1.2 = 1092 g$

3. **a)** $\frac{300}{2500} \times 100 = 12\%$
   b) $\frac{350}{1700} \times 100 = 21\%$ (to the nearest %)

Page 37: Repeated percentage change and finding the original value

1. **a)** $100\% + 56\% = 156\%$
   $156\% = 156 \div 100 = 1.56$

   b) $100\% + 32\% = 132\%$
   $132\% = 132 \div 100 = 1.32$

   c) $100\% - 4\% = 96\%$
   $96\% = 96 \div 100 = 0.96$

   d) $100\% - 21\% = 79\%$
   $79\% = 79 \div 100 = 0.79$

2. $£1200 \times (1.03)^5 = £1391.13$

3. $£20000 \times (1 - 0.08)^{10}$
   $= £20000 \times (0.92)^{10}$
   $= £8687.77$

4. Say original price is x
   $x \times 0.9 = £180$
   $x = £200$

5. Say original price is x
   $x \times 1.08 = £850$
   $x = £787.04$

Page 39: Direct proportion

1. $\times 2 \left(\begin{array}{l} \text{3 pencils : 75p} \\ \text{6 pencils : } \textbf{£1.50} \end{array} \right) \times 2$

2. $\div 2 \left(\begin{array}{l} \text{4 lollipops = 80p} \\ \text{2 lollipops = } \textbf{40p} \end{array} \right) \div 2$

3. $\times 3 \left(\begin{array}{l} \text{60 words = 1 minute} \\ \textbf{180 words} \text{ = 3 minutes} \end{array} \right) \times 3$

4. $\div 3 \left. \begin{array}{l} \text{3 hours = £150} \\ \text{1 hour = £50} \\ \text{5 hours = } \textbf{£250} \end{array} \right\} \begin{array}{l} \div 3 \\ \times 5 \end{array}$

5.

$\div 2$ $\begin{cases} \text{2 pencils} = 44\text{p} \\ \text{1 pencil} = 22\text{p} \\ \text{9 pencils} = \textbf{198p (or £1.98)} \end{cases}$ $\div 2$
$\times 9$ $\qquad\qquad\qquad\qquad\qquad\qquad\quad \times 9$

6.
$\div 4$ $\begin{cases} \text{120 miles} = \text{4 hours} \\ \text{30 miles} = \text{1 hour} \\ \textbf{210 miles} = \text{7 hours} \end{cases}$ $\div 4$
$\times 7$ $\qquad\qquad\qquad\qquad\qquad\qquad \times 7$

7. $A = kB$ $\qquad 24 = k \times 4$ $\qquad 6 = k$
$A = 6 \times 9 = 54$

8. $X = kY$ $\qquad 35 = k \times 7$ $\qquad 5 = k$
$X = 5 \times 9 = 45$

9. $P = kQ$ $\qquad 60 = k \times 120$ $\quad 0.5 = k$
$P = 0.5 \times 100 = 50$

Page 41: Inverse proportion

1. $\div 2$ $\begin{cases} \text{10 people} = \text{20 hours} \\ \text{5 people} = \textbf{40 hours} \end{cases}$ $\times 2$

2. $\times 3$ $\begin{cases} \text{4 builders} = \text{6 hours} \\ \text{12 builders} = \textbf{2 hours} \end{cases}$ $\div 3$

3. $\div 4$ $\begin{cases} \text{4 teachers} = \text{8 hours} \\ \text{1 teacher} = \textbf{32 hours} \end{cases}$ $\times 4$

4. $\div 3$ $\begin{cases} \text{3 friends} = \text{6 days} \\ \text{1 friends} = \text{18 days} \\ \text{2 friends} = \textbf{9 days} \end{cases}$ $\times 3$
$\times 2$ $\qquad\qquad\qquad\qquad\qquad \div 2$

5. $\div 2$ $\begin{cases} \text{2 people} = \text{5 hours} \\ \text{1 person} = \text{10 hours} \\ \text{5 people} = \textbf{2 hours} \end{cases}$ $\times 2$
$\times 5$ $\qquad\qquad\qquad\qquad\qquad \div 5$

6. $\div 2$ $\begin{cases} \text{4 people} = \text{3 hours} \\ \text{2 people} = \text{6 hours} \\ \text{6 people} = \textbf{2 hours} \end{cases}$ $\times 2$
$\times 3$ $\qquad\qquad\qquad\qquad\qquad \div 3$

7. $A = \dfrac{k}{B}$ $\qquad 4 = \dfrac{k}{2}$ $\qquad 8 = k$
$A = \dfrac{8}{8} = 1$

8. $X = \dfrac{k}{Y}$ $\qquad 3 = \dfrac{k}{4}$ $\qquad 12 = k$
$X = \dfrac{12}{2} = 6$

9. $P = \dfrac{k}{Q}$ $\qquad 4 = \dfrac{k}{5}$ $\qquad 20 = k$
$2 = \dfrac{20}{Q}$ $\qquad 2Q = 20$
$Q = 10$

Page 43: Measures of central tendency and spread

1. **a)** 6 $\qquad$ **b)** 5 $\qquad$ **c)** 5
2. **a)** 4 $\qquad$ **b)** 3.5 $\qquad$ **c)** 3
3. 9
4. 4

Page 45: Frequency tables

1. **a)** Qualitative

b)

Colour	Tally	Frequency
Green	ЖЖ III	8
Blue	ЖЖ II	7
Red	ЖЖ II	7
Yellow	ЖЖ IIII	9
		Total = 31

2.

Speed, x mph	Tally	Frequency
$40 < x \leqslant 50$	IIII	4
$50 < x \leqslant 60$	ЖЖ	5
$60 < x \leqslant 70$	ЖЖ II	7
$70 < x \leqslant 80$	IIII	4
		Total = 20

3. **a)**

Temperature	Tally	Frequency
21°C	I	1
22°C		0
23°C	II	2
24°C	III	3
25°C	I	1
		Total = 7

b) 23.4°C **c)** 24°C **d)** 24°C **e)** 4°C

4.

	Sandwich	Hot meal	Total
Porridge	26	10	36
Toast	14	20	34
Total	40	30	70

Page 47: Bar charts and pictograms

1.

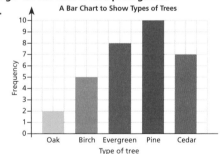

A Bar Chart to Show Types of Trees

2.

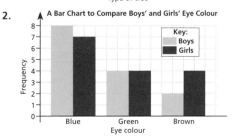

A Bar Chart to Compare Boys' and Girls' Eye Colour

3.

Favourite Sports of Year 8 Students

Badminton	◯◯◯◯
Netball	◯◯◯
Basketball	◯◯◯◯◯
Table tennis	◯
Key: ◯ = 5	

4.

Number of Cupcakes Sold

Monday	🧁🧁🧁🧁🧁
Tuesday	🧁🧁🧁
Wednesday	🧁🧁🧁
Thursday	🧁🧁🧁🧁
Friday	🧁🧁🧁🧁🧁
Saturday	🧁🧁🧁🧁🧁🧁🧁🧁🧁
Key: 🧁 = 6 cupcakes	

Page 49: Pie charts and scatter graphs

1. a)

Colour	Frequency	Fraction	Angle
White	9	$\frac{9}{36}$	90°
Green	20	$\frac{20}{36}$	200°
Red	7	$\frac{7}{36}$	70°

b)

2. a) $\frac{60}{360} \times 48 = 8$ **b)** $\frac{180}{360} \times 48 = 24$

c) $\frac{120}{360} \times 48 = 16$

3. a)

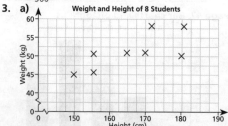

Weight and Height of 8 Students

b) Weak positive correlation. As height increases, weight increases.

4. a)

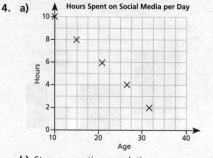

Hours Spent on Social Media per Day

b) Strong negative correlation

Page 51: Interpreting statistical representations

1. a) 10   **b)** 4   **c)** 15 − 12 = 3

d) Peanut butter

e) 4 + 15 + 12 + 24 + 10 + 10 = 75

2. The median is more reliable because it will not be affected by the very large value of £2435 compared to the rest of the data.

3. The mode should be used because it is the only measure of central tendency that can be used for qualitative data.

4. City D should be chosen because the mean maximum daily temperature is greater than in city C, and the mean provides information on the average daily temperature in March.

Page 53: Properties of polygons

1.

Quadrilateral	Image	Sides	Angles
Square		• Four equal sides • Opposite sides are parallel	• All equal angles (90°)
Rectangle		• Two pairs of equal sides • Opposite sides are parallel	• All equal angles (90°)
Parallelogram		• Two pairs of equal sides • Opposite sides are parallel	• Two opposite pairs of equal angles
Rhombus		• Four equal sides • Opposite sides are parallel	• Two opposite pairs of equal angles
Kite		• Two pairs of equal sides	• One opposite pair of equal angles
Trapezium		• One pair of parallel sides	• The two angles at the end of each non-parallel side add to 180°

2. 100° + 95° + 60° = 255°

360° − 255° = 105°

$x = 105°$

3. Columns should be completed as follows.

Equilateral triangle	Isosceles triangle	Scalene triangle
• All sides are equal length • All angles are equal size (60°)	• Two sides are equal length • Two equal angles	• No equal sides • No equal angles

Acute triangle	Right triangle	Obtuse triangle
• Has three angles that are all less than 90°	• Has one angle that equals 90°	• Has one angle that is greater than 90°

4. 70° + 50° = 120°

180° − 120° = 60°

$a = 60°$

Page 55: Solving problems with perimeter and area

1. a) $10 + 6 + 8 = 24\,\text{cm}$ b) $\frac{8 \times 6}{2} = 24\,\text{cm}^2$

2. $15 = \frac{x \times 5}{2}$ $30 = 5x$ $6 = x$
   6 cm

3. a) $12 + 12 + 8 + 8 = 40\,\text{cm}$
   b) $12 \times 6 = 72\,\text{cm}^2$

4. $11 + 13 + 23 + 9 = 56\,\text{cm}$

5. $\frac{7+9}{2} \times 8 = 64\,\text{cm}^2$

6. Example method:

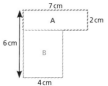

Area of rectangle A = $7 \times 2 = 14\,\text{cm}^2$
Unknown length of rectangle B = $6 - 2 = 4\,\text{cm}$
Area of rectangle B = $4 \times 4 = 16\,\text{cm}^2$
Area of compound shape = $14 + 16 = 30\,\text{cm}^2$

Page 57: Area and circumference of a circle

1. a) 37.7 cm (1 d.p.)   b) 44.0 cm (1 d.p.)
2. a) 113.1 cm² (1 d.p.) b) 153.9 cm² (1 d.p.)
3. 8.0 cm (1 d.p.)
4. 22.9 cm (1 d.p.)
5. a) 3.9 cm (1 d.p.)   b) 7.8 cm (1 d.p.)
   c) 24.5 cm or 24.6 cm (1 d.p.)

Page 59: Surface area

1. a) Area of each face: Front $3 \times 2 = 6$; Back
   $3 \times 2 = 6$; Top $5 \times 2 = 10$; Bottom $5 \times 2 =$
   10; Left $5 \times 3 = 15$; Right $5 \times 3 = 15$
   Total surface area = 62 cm²
   b) Area of each face: Front $5 \times 6 = 30$; Back
   $5 \times 6 = 30$; Top $6 \times 8 = 48$; Bottom
   $6 \times 8 = 48$; Left $5 \times 8 = 40$; Right $5 \times 8 = 40$
   Total surface area = 236 cm²

2. a) Area of each face: Front $\frac{4 \times 3}{2} = 6$; Back
   $\frac{4 \times 3}{2} = 6$; Bottom $3 \times 5 = 15$; Left $4 \times 5 = 20$;
   Right (sloping) $5 \times 5 = 25$
   Total surface area = 72 cm²
   b) Area of each face: Front $\frac{6 \times 3}{2} = 9$; Back
   $\frac{6 \times 3}{2} = 9$; Bottom $10 \times 6 = 60$; Left (sloping)
   $7 \times 10 = 70$; Right $10 \times 3 = 30$
   Total surface area = 178 cm²

3. a) Area of one circular face = $\pi \times 5^2 = 25\pi$
   Area of both circular faces = $25\pi \times 2 = 50\pi$
   Area of rectangular face = $10\pi \times 12 = 120\pi$
   Total surface area = $50\pi + 120\pi = 170\pi$
   = 534.07 cm²

b) Area of one circular face = $\pi \times 5^2 = 25\pi$
   Area of both circular faces = $25\pi \times 2 = 50\pi$
   Area of rectangular face = $10\pi \times 10 = 100\pi$
   Total surface area = $50\pi + 100\pi = 150\pi$
   = 471.24 cm²

Page 61: Solving problems with volume

1. a) $l = 80 \div 10 = 8\,\text{cm}$ b) $l = 45 \div 9 = 5\,\text{cm}$
   c) $l = 600 \div 30 = 20\,\text{cm}$ d) $l = 36 \div 12 = 3\,\text{m}$
2. $h = 240 \div 24 = 10\,\text{cm}$
3. a) $l = 30 \div 6 = 5\,\text{cm}$ b) $l = 48 \div 12 = 4\,\text{mm}$
4. a) $h = 54\pi \div 6\pi = 9\,\text{m}$
   b) $h = 66\pi \div 11\pi = 6\,\text{cm}$

Page 63: Angle properties

For some questions, other reasons are possible.

1. a) $x = 65°$, angles in a right angle sum to 90°
   b) $v = 140°$, vertically opposite angles are equal
   $w = 40°$, vertically opposite angles are equal
   c) $v = 55°$, angles on a straight line sum to 180°
   d) $a = 80°$, angles on a straight line sum to 180°
   $b = 120°$, angles on a straight line sum to 180°
   $c = 60°$, vertically opposite angles are equal
   e) $2n = 72°$, $3n = 108°$, angles on a straight
   line sum to 180°

2. a) Base angles = 55°, base angles of an
   isosceles triangle are equal
   $d = 70°$, angles in a triangle sum to 180°
   b) $e = 62°$, angles in a triangle sum to 180°
   c) $f = 140°$, angles on a straight line sum to 180°
   $g = 25°$, angles in a triangle sum to 180°
   d) Top angle of triangle = 80°, vertically
   opposite angles are equal
   $h = 50°$, base angles of an isosceles triangle
   are equal
   e) Angles in an equilateral triangle are 60°
   $i = 120°$, angles on a straight line sum to 180°
   $j = 60°$, vertically opposite angles are equal
   f) $n = 100°$, opposite angles in a kite
   $m = 110°$, angles in a quadrilateral sum to 360°
   g) $p = 100°$, top angles of an isosceles
   trapezium are equal
   $q = r = 80°$, base angles of an isosceles
   trapezium are equal, angles in a
   quadrilateral sum to 360°
   h) $t = 45°$, opposite angles in a parallelogram
   are equal
   $s = u = 135°$, opposite angles in a
   parallelogram are equal, angles in a
   quadrilateral sum to 360°

Page 65: Angles in parallel lines

For some questions, other reasons are possible.

1. **a)** $x = 40°$ Alternate angles

   $y = 140°$ Angles on a straight line sum to 180°

   b) $a = 105°$ Corresponding angles

   $b = 105°$ Vertically opposite angles

2. **a)** $x = 65°$, corresponding angles

   $f = 115°$, angles on a straight line sum to 180°

   b) $x = 45°$, corresponding angles

   $g = 45°$, vertically opposite angles

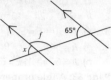

3.

Label the angles corresponding to a.

This shows that $a + b = 180°$

Label all the angles vertically opposite to either a or b.

Label all the angles corresponding to b.

Use the fact that $a + b = 180°$ to label the rest of the angles.

In the parallelogram, opposite angles are equal.

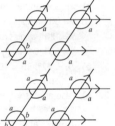

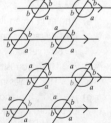

Page 67: Angles in polygons

1. **a)** $a = 135°$; $b = 95°$; $c = 110°$;

   $d = 360° - 70° - 90° - 85° - 45° = 70°$;

   $e = 110°$

   b) $g = 65°$; $h = 50°$; $k = 115°$; $m = 130°$; $n = 115°$

2. Exterior angle 45°; interior angle 135°

3. 12 sides

4. 900°

5. $x = 360° - 90° - 120° = 150°$

6. $y = 360° - 60° - 108° = 192°$

Page 69: Using triangles in constructions

Accurate constructions should be drawn.

Page 71: Perpendicular bisector and perpendicular line through a point

Accurate constructions should be drawn.

Page 73: Angle bisectors

Accurate constructions should be drawn.

Pages 74–77: Mixed questions

1. **a)** 12 600   **b)** 1.02   **c)** 0.009 18

2.

Fraction	Decimal	Percentage
$\frac{2}{5}$	0.4	40%
$\frac{9}{20}$	0.45	45%
$\frac{3}{4}$	0.75	75%
$\frac{7}{8}$	0.875	87.5%

3. **a)** 1.6   **b)** 0   **c)** 1.5   **d)** 4

4. **a)** Qualitative data

   b)

Transport	Tally	Frequency
Walk	ЖТ ЖТ III	13
Bus	ЖТ II	7
Bike	ЖТ	5
Car	IIII	4
Train	I	1
		Total = 30

5. **a)** Arithmetic   **b)** $6n - 4$

6. $y = 2x - 3$

7. **a)** $y = -2$ **b)** $x = 4$ **c)** $y = x$ **d)** $y = 2x + 1$

8. **a)** $x = 6$ **b)** $x = \frac{1}{2}$ **c)** $x = 12$ **d)** $x = 22$

9. 4245

10. **a)** 62   **b)** Ham and pineapple   **c)** 7

11. $x + 17$

12. **a)**

Answer	Frequency	Fraction	Angle
Yes	16	$\frac{16}{18}$	320°
No	2	$\frac{2}{18}$	40°

   b)

13. **a)** $x = -3$ **b)** $x = 1$

14. **a)** £55.24   **b)** £19 200   **c)** £405

15. $x = 6.5$

16. $2y - x + 6 = 0$

17. £246 000

18. 64 m

19. **a)** 678.6 cm²   **b)** 21.0 cm

20. **a)** 54   **b)** 3